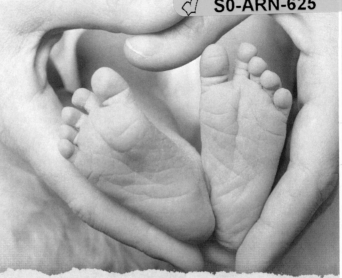

HOW DEEP

A Mother's Love...

A DEVOTIONAL JOURNEY

Freeman-Smith, a division of Worthy Media, Inc.

134 Franklin Road, Suite 200, Brentwood, Tennessee 37027

The quoted ideas expressed in this book (but not Scripture verses) are not, in all cases, exact quotations, as some have been edited for clarity and brevity. In all cases, the author has attempted to maintain the speaker's original intent. In some cases, quoted material for this book was obtained from secondary sources, primarily print media. While every effort was made to ensure the accuracy of these sources, the accuracy cannot be guaranteed. For additions, deletions, corrections, or clarifications in future editions of this text, please write Freeman-Smith.

Scripture quotations are taken from:

The Holy Bible, King James Version (KJV)

The Holy Bible, New International Version (NIV) Copyright © 1973, 1978, 1984, by International Bible Society. Used by permission of Zondervan Publishing House. All rights reserved.

The Holy Bible, New King James Version (NKJV) Copyright © 1982 by Thomas Nelson, Inc. Used by permission.

Holy Bible, New Living Translation, (NLT) copyright © 1996. Used by permission of Tyndale House Publishers, Inc., Wheaton, Illinois 60189. All rights reserved.

The Message (MSG)- This edition issued by contractual arrangement with NavPress, a division of The Navigators, U.S.A. Originally published by NavPress in English as THE MESSAGE: The Bible in Contemporary Language copyright 2002-2003 by Eugene Peterson. All rights reserved.

New Century Version®. (NCV) Copyright © 1987, 1988, 1991 by Word Publishing, a division of Thomas Nelson, Inc. All rights reserved. Used by permission.

The New American Standard Bible®, (NASB) Copyright © 1960, 1962, 1963, 1968, 1971, 1972, 1973, 1975, 1977, 1995 by The Lockman Foundation. Used by permission.

The Holman Christian Standard Bible™ (HCSB) Copyright © 1999, 2000, 2001 by Holman Bible Publishers. Used by permission.

Cover Design by Kim Russell / Wahoo Designs

Page Layout by Bart Dawson

ISBN 978-1-60587-354-1

Printed in the United States of America

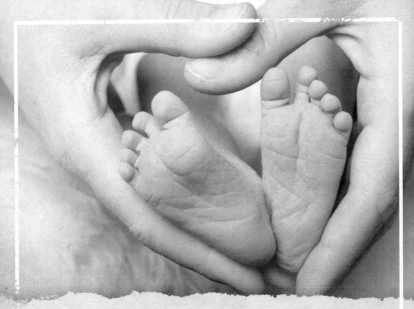

HOW DEEP

A Mother's Love...

A DEVOTIONAL JOURNEY

Table of Contents

Introduction

Because you're reading this book, you probably answer to the name "Mom," "Mother," "Mommy," or some variation thereof—if so, congratulations. As a loving mother, you have been blessed by your children and by your creator.

Your life here on earth is an all-too-brief journey from the cradle to the grave. When you make that journey with God—and when you encourage your family members to do the same—you will avail yourself of the peace and abundance that God offers to those who invite Him into their hearts.

As a mother, you are keenly aware of the priceless treasure that the Creator has entrusted to your care; that treasure, of course, is your family. And as a Christian, you're also aware of another incalculable treasure that is yours for the asking: the gift of eternal life that was purchased by God's only begotten Son on the cross at Calvary. This devotional book serves as an inspirational reminder of these and other blessings that you, as a Christian mom, can savor for a lifetime and beyond.

Motherhood is both a priceless gift from God and an unrelenting responsibility. The ideas on these pages are intended to remind you that when it comes to the tough job of being a responsible mother, you and God, working together, are destined to do great things for your kids and for the world.

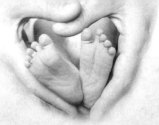

A Mother's Love

Her children rise up and call her blessed.

Proverbs 31:28 NKJV

Few things in life are as precious or as enduring as a mother's love. Our mothers give us life, and they care for us. They nurture us when we are sick and encourage us when we're brokenhearted. Indeed, a mother's love is both powerful and priceless.

Christ showed His love for us on the cross, and, as Christians, we are called upon to return Christ's love by sharing it. Sometimes love is easy (puppies and sleeping children come to mind), and sometimes love is hard (fallible human beings come to mind). But God's Word is clear: We are to love our families and our neighbors without reservation or condition.

As a caring mother, you are not only shaping the lives of your loved ones, you are also, in a very real sense, reshaping eternity. It's a big job, a job so big, in fact, that God saw fit to entrust it to some of the most important people in His kingdom: loving moms like you.

More from God's Word

I pray that you, being rooted and firmly established in love, may be able to comprehend with all the saints what is the breadth and width, height and depth, and to know the Messiah's love that surpasses knowledge, so you may be filled with all the fullness of God.

Ephesians 3:17-19 HCSB

If I speak the languages of men and of angels, but do not have love, I am a sounding gong or a clanging cymbal.

1 Corinthians 13:1 HCSB

Dear friends, if God loved us in this way, we also must love one another.

1 John 4:11 HCSB

We love because He first loved us.

1 John 4:19 HCSB

Hatred stirs up conflicts, but love covers all offenses.

Proverbs 10:12 HCSB

MY WEEK ON THE GO

monday _____
_____
_____

tuesday _____
_____
_____

wednesday _____
_____
_____

thursday _____
_____
_____

friday _____
_____
_____

saturday _____
_____
_____

sunday _____
_____
_____

More Ideas for Your Journey

Mothers must model the tenderness we need. Our world can't find it anywhere else.

Charles Swindoll

The loveliest masterpiece of the heart of God is the heart of a mother.

St. Thérèse of Lisieux

As a mother, my job is to take care of the possible and trust God with the impossible.

Ruth Bell Graham

A Mother's Prayer

Dear Lord, Your love for me endures forever; so, too, does my love for my own children. Help me to use my role as a mother, Lord, to lavish love upon these precious souls You have placed in my care. Amen

Who's First?

You shall have no other gods before Me.

Exodus 20:3 NKJV

As you think about the nature of your relationship with God, remember this: you will always have some type of relationship with Him—it is inevitable that your life must be lived in relationship to God. The question is not if you will have a relationship with Him; the burning question is whether or not that relationship will be one that seeks to honor Him.

Are you willing to place God first in your life? And, are you willing to welcome God's Son into your heart? Unless you can honestly answer these questions with a resounding yes, then your relationship with God isn't what it could be or should be. Thankfully, God is always available, He's always ready to forgive, and He's waiting to hear from you now. The rest, of course, is up to you.

More from God's Word

Be careful not to forget the Lord.

Deuteronomy 6:12 HCSB

It is good to give thanks to the Lord, and to sing praises to Your name, O Most High; to declare Your lovingkindness in the morning, and Your faithfulness every night.

Psalm 92:1-2 NKJV

Love the Lord your God with all your heart, with all your soul, and with all your strength.

Deuteronomy 6:5 HCSB

The Devil said to Him, "I will give You their splendor and all this authority, because it has been given over to me, and I can give it to anyone I want. If You, then, will worship me, all will be Yours." And Jesus answered him, "It is written: You shall worship the Lord your God, and Him alone you shall serve."

Luke 4:6-8 HCSB

The thing you should want most is God's kingdom and doing what God wants. Then all these other things you need will be given to you.

Matthew 6:33 NCV

More Ideas for Your Journey

Our ultimate aim in life is not to be healthy, wealthy, prosperous, or problem free. Our ultimate aim in life is to bring glory to God.

Anne Graham Lotz

When all else is gone, God is still left. Nothing changes Him.

Hannah Whitall Smith

To God be the glory, great things He has done; / So loved He the world that He gave us His Son.

Fanny Crosby

A Mother's Prayer

Dear Lord, Your love is eternal and Your laws are everlasting. When I obey Your commandments, I am blessed. Today, I invite You to reign over every corner of my heart. I will have faith in You, Father. I will sense Your presence; I will accept Your love; I will trust Your will; and I will praise You for the Savior of my life: Your Son Jesus. Amen

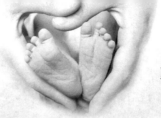

What Kind of Example?

You should be an example to the believers in speech, in conduct, in love, in faith, in purity.

1 Timothy 4:12 HCSB

Our children learn from the lessons we teach and the lives we live, but not necessarily in that order. As mothers, we serve as unforgettable role models for our children and grandchildren. Hopefully, the lives we lead and the choices we make will serve as enduring examples of the spiritual abundance that is available to all who worship God and obey His commandments.

What kind of example are you? Are you the kind of mother whose life serves as a genuine example of patience and righteousness? Are you a woman whose behavior serves as a positive role model for others? Are you the kind of mom whose actions, day in and day out, are based upon kindness, faithfulness, and a sincere love for the Lord? If so, you are not only blessed by God, but you are also a powerful force for good in a world that desperately needs positive influences such as yours.

Corrie ten Boom advised, "Don't worry about what you do not understand. Worry about what you do understand in the Bible but do not live by." And that's sound advice because our families and friends are watching . . . and so, for that matter, is God.

More from God's Word

Do everything without grumbling and arguing, so that you may be blameless and pure.

Philippians 2:14–15 HCSB

Set an example of good works yourself, with integrity and dignity in your teaching.

Titus 2:7 HCSB

For the kingdom of God is not in talk but in power.

1 Corinthians 4:20 HCSB

Therefore since we also have such a large cloud of witnesses surrounding us, let us lay aside every weight and the sin that so easily ensnares us, and run with endurance the race that lies before us.

Hebrews 12:1 HCSB

More Ideas for Your Journey

In your desire to share the gospel, you may be the only Jesus someone else will ever meet. Be real and be involved with people.

Barbara Johnson

Living life with a consistent spiritual walk deeply influences those we love most.

Vonette Bright

Among the most joyful people I have known have been some who seem to have had no human reason for joy. The sweet fragrance of Christ has shown through their lives.

Elisabeth Elliot

A Mother's Prayer

Lord, make me a worthy example to my family and friends. And, let my words and my deeds serve as a testimony to the changes You have made in my life. Let me praise You, Father, by following in the footsteps of Your Son, and let others see Him through me. Amen

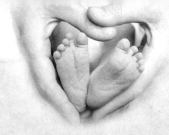

Very Big Plans

Teach me to do Your will, for You are my God. May Your gracious Spirit lead me on level ground.

Psalm 143:10 HCSB

The Bible makes it clear: God has plans—very big plans—for you and your family. But He won't force His plans upon you—if you wish to experience the abundance that God has in store, you must be willing to accept His will and follow His Son.

As Christians, you and your family members should ask yourselves this question: "How closely can we make our plans match God's plans?" The more closely you manage to follow the path that God intends for your lives, the better.

Do you and your loved ones have questions or concerns about the future? Take them to God in prayer. Do you have hopes and expectations? Talk to God about your dreams. Are you and your family members carefully planning for the days and weeks ahead? Consult God as you establish your priorities. Turn every concern over to your Heavenly Father, and sincerely seek His guidance—prayerfully, earnestly, and often. Then, listen for His answers . . . and trust the answers that He gives.

More from God's Word

We know that all things work together for the good of those who love God: those who are called according to His purpose.

Romans 8:28 HCSB

But as for you, you meant evil against me; but God meant it for good, in order to bring it about as it is this day, to save many people alive.

Genesis 50:20 NKJV

"For My thoughts are not your thoughts, nor are your ways My ways," says the LORD. "For as the heavens are higher than the earth, so are My ways higher than your ways, and My thoughts than your thoughts."

Isaiah 55:8-9 NKJV

"I say this because I know what I am planning for you," says the Lord. "I have good plans for you, not plans to hurt you. I will give you hope and a good future."

Jeremiah 29:11 NCV

More Ideas for Your Journey

God prepared a plan for your life alone—and neither man nor the devil can destroy that plan.

Kay Arthur

The God who created and numbers the stars in the heavens also numbers the hairs of my head. He pays attention to very big things and to very small ones. What matters to me matters to Him, and that changes my life.

Elisabeth Elliot

We will stand amazed to see the topside of the tapestry and how God beautifully embroidered each circumstance into a pattern for our good and His glory.

Joni Eareckson Tada

A Mother's Prayer

Lord, You have a plan for my life that is grander than I can imagine. Let Your purposes be my purposes. Let Your will be my will. When I am confused, give me clarity. When I am frightened, give me courage. Let me be Your faithful servant, always seeking Your guidance for my life. And, let me always be a shining beacon for Your Son today and every day that I live. Amen

A Rule That's Golden

Just as you want others to do for you, do the same for them.

Luke 6:31 HCSB

The words of Matthew 7:12 remind us that, as believers in Christ, we are commanded to treat others as we wish to be treated. This commandment is, indeed, the Golden Rule for Christians of every generation. When we weave the thread of kindness into the very fabric of our lives, we give glory to the One who gave His life for ours.

Because we are imperfect human beings, we are, on occasion, selfish, thoughtless, or cruel. But God commands us to behave otherwise. He teaches us to rise above our own imperfections and to treat others with unselfishness and love. When we observe God's Golden Rule, we help build His kingdom here on earth. And, when we share the love of Christ, we share a priceless gift; may we share it today and every day that we live.

More Ideas for Your Journey

I have discovered that when I please Christ, I end up inadvertently serving others far more effectively.

Beth Moore

The Golden Rule starts at home, but it should never stop there.

Marie T. Freeman

It is one of the most beautiful compensations of life that no one can sincerely try to help another without helping herself.

Barbara Johnson

A Mother's Prayer

Lord, in all aspects of my life, let me treat others as I wish to be treated. The Golden Rule is Your rule, Father; let me make it mine. Amen

Behaving Differently

So don't get tired of doing what is good. Don't get discouraged and give up, for we will reap a harvest of blessing at the appropriate time.

Galatians 6:9 NLT

Oswald Chambers, the author of the Christian classic, *My Utmost for His Highest*, advised, "Never support an experience which does not have God as its source, and faith in God as its result." These words serve as a powerful reminder that, as Christians, we are called to walk with God and obey His commandments. But, we live in a world that presents countless temptations for adults and even more temptations for our children.

We Christians, when confronted with sin, have clear instructions: walk—or better yet run—in the opposite direction. When we do, we reap the blessings that God has promised to all those who live according to His will and His Word.

More from God's Word

As obedient children, do not be conformed to the desires of your former ignorance but, as the One who called you is holy, you also are to be holy in all your conduct.

1 Peter 1:14-15 HCSB

For this very reason, make every effort to supplement your faith with goodness, goodness with knowledge, knowledge with self-control, self-control with endurance, endurance with godliness.

2 Peter 1:5-6 HCSB

Therefore as you have received Christ Jesus the Lord, walk in Him.

Colossians 2:6 HCSB

Who is wise and understanding among you? He should show his works by good conduct with wisdom's gentleness.

James 3:13 HCSB

Even a young man is known by his actions—by whether his behavior is pure and upright.

Proverbs 20:11 HCSB

More Ideas for Your Journey

Although God causes all things to work together for good for His children, He still holds us accountable for our behavior.

Kay Arthur

Either God's Word keeps you from sin, or sin keeps you from God's Word.

Corrie ten Boom

There may be no trumpet sound or loud applause when we make a right decision, just a calm sense of resolution and peace.

Gloria Gaither

A Mother's Prayer

Lord, there is a right way and a wrong way to live. Let me live according to Your rules, not the world's rules. Your path is right for me, God; let me follow it every day of my life. Amen

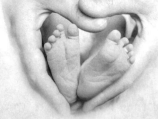

His Joy and Yours

I have spoken these things to you so that My joy may be in you and your joy may be complete.

John 15:11 HCSB

Are you a mom whose smile is evident for all to see? If so, congratulations: your joyful spirit serves as a powerful example to your family and friends. And because of your attitude, you may be assured that your children will indeed "rise up" and call you blessed (Proverbs 31:28).

Sometimes, amid the inevitable hustle and bustle of life here on earth, you may forfeit—albeit temporarily—the joy that God intends for you to experience and to share. But even on life's most difficult days, you may rest assured that God is in His heaven, and He still cares for you.

God's plan for you and your family includes heaping helpings of abundance and joy. Claim them. And remember that Christ offers you and your family priceless gifts: His abundance, His peace, and His joy. Accept those gifts and share them freely, just as Christ has freely shared Himself with you.

More from God's Word

Rejoice in the Lord always. I will say it again: Rejoice!

Philippians 4:4 HCSB

Delight yourself also in the Lord, and He shall give you the desires of your heart.

Psalm 37:4 NKJV

Make me hear joy and gladness.

Psalm 51:8 NKJV

Weeping may spend the night, but there is joy in the morning.

Psalm 30:5 HCSB

The Lord reigns; let the earth rejoice.

Psalm 97:1 NKJV

More Ideas for Your Journey

What is your focus today? Joy comes when it is Jesus first, others second…then you.

Kay Arthur

Finding joy means first of all finding Jesus.

Jill Briscoe

The Christian lifestyle is not one of legalistic do's and don'ts, but one that is positive, attractive, and joyful.

Vonette Bright

A Mother's Prayer

Dear Lord, You have given me so many blessings; let me celebrate Your gifts. Make me thankful, loving, responsible, and wise. I praise You, Father, for the gift of Your Son and for the priceless gift of salvation. Make me be a joyful Christian and a worthy example to my loved ones, today and every day. Amen

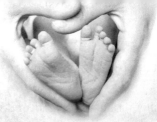

You and Your Family

Unless the Lord builds a house, its builders labor over it in vain; unless the Lord watches over a city, the watchman stays alert in vain.

Psalm 127:1 HCSB

As every mother knows, family life is a mixture of conversations, mediations, irritations, deliberations, commiserations, frustrations, negotiations, and celebrations. In other words, the life of the typical mom is incredibly varied.

Certainly, in the life of every family, there are moments of frustration and disappointment. Lots of them. But, for those who are lucky enough to live in the presence of a close-knit, caring clan, the rewards far outweigh the frustrations.

No family is perfect, and neither is yours. But, despite the inevitable challenges and occasional hurt feelings of family life, your clan is God's gift to you. That little band of men, women, kids, and babies is a priceless treasure on temporary loan from the Father above. Give thanks to the Giver for the gift of family.

More Ideas for Your Journey

There is so much compassion and understanding that is gained when we've experienced God's grace firsthand within our own families.

Lisa Whelchel

For whatever life holds for you and your family in the coming days, weave the unfailing fabric of God's Word through your heart and mind. It will hold strong, even if the rest of life unravels.

Gigi Graham Tchividjian

One way or the other, God, who thought up the family in the first place, has the very best idea of how to bring sense to the chaos of broken relationships we see all around us. I really believe that if I remain still and listen a lot, He will share some solutions with me so I can share them with others.

Jill Briscoe

A Mother's Prayer

Lord, You have given me a family to love and to care for. Thank You, Father. I will love all the members of my family despite their imperfections. Let them love me, Dear Lord, despite mine. Amen

The Spiritual Journey

But grow in the grace and knowledge of our Lord and Savior Jesus Christ. To Him be the glory both now and to the day of eternity.

2 Peter 3:18 HCSB

The journey toward spiritual maturity lasts a lifetime: As Christian mothers, we can and should continue to grow in the love and the knowledge of our Savior as long as we live. When we cease to grow, either emotionally or spiritually, we do ourselves and our loved ones a profound disservice. But, if we study God's Word, if we obey His commandments, and if we live in the center of His will, we will not be "stagnant" believers; we will, instead, be growing Christians . . . and that's exactly what God wants for our lives.

Many of life's most important lessons are painful to learn. During times of heartbreak and hardship, God stands ready to protect us. As Psalm 147 promises, "He heals the brokenhearted and bandages their wounds" (NCV). In His own time and according to His master plan, God will heal us if we invite Him into our hearts.

Spiritual growth need not take place only in times of adversity. We should seek to grow in our relationship with the Lord through every season of our lives, through happy times and hard times, through times of celebration and times of pain.

In those quiet moments when we open our hearts to God, the One who made us keeps remaking us. He gives us direction, perspective, wisdom, and courage. And of course, the appropriate moment to accept those spiritual gifts is always the present one.

More from God's Word

I want their hearts to be encouraged and joined together in love, so that they may have all the riches of assured understanding, and have the knowledge of God's mystery—Christ.

Colossians 2:2 HCSB

Therefore, leaving the elementary message about the Messiah, let us go on to maturity.

Hebrews 6:1 HCSB

Now may the God of hope fill you with all joy and peace in believing, so that you may overflow with hope by the power of the Holy Spirit.

Romans 15:13 HCSB

More Ideas for Your Journey

There is wonderful freedom and joy in coming to recognize that the fun is in the becoming.

Gloria Gaither

Our heavenly Father knows to place us where we may learn lessons impossible anywhere else. He has neither misplaced nor displaced us.

Elisabeth Elliot

Kindness in this world will do much to help others, not only to come into the light, but also to grow in grace day by day.

Fanny Crosby

A Mother's Prayer

Dear Lord, the Bible tells me that You are at work in my life, continuing to help me grow and to mature in my faith. Show me Your wisdom, Father, and let me live according to Your Word and Your will. Amen

Controlling Your Temper

My dear brothers and sisters, be quick to listen, slow to speak, and slow to get angry. Your anger can never make things right in God's sight.

James 1:19-20 NLT

Motherhood is vastly rewarding, but every mother knows that it can be, at times, frustrating. No family is perfect, and even the most loving mother's patience can, on occasion, wear thin.

Your temper is either your master or your servant. Either you control it, or it controls you. And the extent to which you allow anger to rule your life will determine, to a surprising degree, the quality of your relationships with others and your relationship with God.

If you've allowed anger to become a regular visitor at your house, you should pray for wisdom, for patience, and for a heart that is so filled with forgiveness that it contains no room for bitterness. God will help you terminate your tantrums if you ask Him to—and that's a good thing because anger and peace cannot coexist in the same mind.

So the next time you're tempted to lose your temper over the minor inconveniences of life, don't. Turn away from anger, hatred, bitterness and regret. Turn instead to God. He's waiting with open arms . . . patiently.

More from God's Word

But now you must also put away all the following: anger, wrath, malice, slander, and filthy language from your mouth.

Colossians 3:8 HCSB

Don't let your spirit rush to be angry, for anger abides in the heart of fools.

Ecclesiastes 7:9 HCSB

All bitterness, anger and wrath, insult and slander must be removed from you, along with all wickedness. And be kind and compassionate to one another, forgiving one another, just as God also forgave you in Christ.

Ephesians 4:31-32 HCSB

More Ideas for Your Journey

Anger is the noise of the soul; the unseen irritant of the heart; the relentless invader of silence.

Max Lucado

When you strike out in anger, you may miss the other person, but you will always hit yourself.

Jim Gallery

Anger unresolved will only bring you woe.

Kay Arthur

A Mother's Prayer

Lord, when I become angry, help me to remember that You offer me peace. Let me turn to You for wisdom, for patience, and for the peace that only You can give. Amen

He's Here

Draw near to God, and He will draw near to you.

James 4:8 HCSB

If you are a busy mother with more obligations than you have time to count, you know all too well that the demands of everyday life can, on occasion, seem overwhelming. Thankfully, even on the days when you feel overburdened, overworked, overstressed and under-appreciated, God is trying to get His message through . . . your job is to listen.

Are you tired, discouraged, or fearful? Be comforted because God is with you. Are you confused? Listen to the quiet voice of your Heavenly Father. Are you bitter? Talk with God and seek His guidance. In whatever condition you find yourself—whether you are happy or sad, victorious or vanquished, troubled or triumphant—carve out moments of silent solitude to celebrate God's gifts and to experience His presence.

The familiar words of Psalm 46:10 remind us to be still before the Creator. When we do, we encounter the awesome presence of our loving Heavenly Father, and we are comforted in the knowledge that God is not just near. He is here.

More from God's Word

The Lord is near all who call out to Him, all who call out to Him with integrity. He fulfills the desires of those who fear Him; He hears their cry for help and saves them.

Psalm 145:18-19 HCSB

No, I will not abandon you as orphans—I will come to you.

John 14:18 NLT

Again, this is God's command: to believe in his personally named Son, Jesus Christ. He told us to love each other, in line with the original command. As we keep his commands, we live deeply and surely in him, and he lives in us. And this is how we experience his deep and abiding presence in us: by the Spirit he gave us.

1 John 3:23-24 MSG

Fear not, for I am with you; Be not dismayed, for I am your God. I will strengthen you.

Isaiah 41:10 NKJV

More Ideas for Your Journey

Our souls were made to live in an upper atmosphere, and we stifle and choke if we live on any lower level. Our eyes were made to look off from these heavenly heights, and our vision is distorted by any lower gazing.

Hannah Whitall Smith

If your heart has grown cold, it is because you have moved away from the fire of His presence.

Beth Moore

If you want to hear God's voice clearly and you are uncertain, then remain in His presence until He changes that uncertainty. Often, much can happen during this waiting for the Lord. Sometimes, he changes pride into humility, doubt into faith and peace.

Corrie ten Boom

A Mother's Prayer

Dear Lord, You are with me when I am strong and when I am weak. You never leave my side, even when it seems to me that You are far away. Today and every day, let me trust Your promises and let me feel Your love. Amen

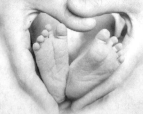

Devotion 12

Proper Perspective

All I'm doing right now, friends, is showing how these things pertain to Apollos and me so that you will learn restraint and not rush into making judgments without knowing all the facts. It is important to look at things from God's point of view. I would rather not see you inflating or deflating reputations based on mere hearsay.

1 Corinthians 4:6 MSG

Even if you're the world's most thoughtful mom, you may, from time to time, lose perspective—it happens on those days when life seems out of balance and the pressures of motherhood seem overwhelming. What's needed is a fresh perspective, a restored sense of balance . . . and God.

If a temporary loss of perspective has left you worried, exhausted or both, it's time to readjust your thought patterns. Negative thoughts are habit-forming; thankfully, so are positive ones. With practice, you can form the habit of focusing on God's priorities and your possibilities. When you do, you'll spend less time fretting about your challenges and more time praising God for His gifts.

So today and every day hereafter, pray for a sense of balance and perspective. And remember: your thoughts are intensely powerful things, so handle them with care.

More Ideas for Your Journey

Instead of being frustrated and overwhelmed by all that is going on in our world, go to the Lord and ask Him to give you His eternal perspective.

Kay Arthur

Attitude is the mind's paintbrush; it can color any situation.

Barbara Johnson

A Mother's Prayer

Dear Lord, when the pace of my life becomes frantic, slow me down and give me perspective. Give me the wisdom to realize that the problems of today are only temporary but that Your love is eternal. When I become discouraged, keep me steady and sure, so that I might do Your will here on earth and then live with You forever in heaven. Amen

Family Worship

I rejoiced with those who said to me, "Let us go to the house of the Lord."

Psalm 122:1 HCSB

When you insist that your family is to worship God, you are to be praised. By worshipping your Creator—and by teaching your children to do likewise—you make a powerful statement about the place that God occupies in your life.

Ours is a society in which too many parents have abandoned the moral leadership of their families, often with tragic consequences. People who neglect to worship God, either thoughtlessly or intentionally, invite untold suffering into their own lives and into the lives of their loved ones.

Every day provides opportunities to put God where He belongs: at the center of our hearts. May we worship Him, and only Him, always. And, may we encourage the members of our family to do the same.

More from God's Word

So that at the name of Jesus every knee should bow—of those who are in heaven and on earth and under the earth—and every tongue should confess that Jesus Christ is Lord, to the glory of God the Father.

Philippians 2:10-11 HCSB

Worship the Lord your God and . . . serve Him only.

Matthew 4:10 HCSB

If anyone is thirsty, he should come to Me and drink!

John 7:37 HCSB

But an hour is coming, and is now here, when the true worshipers will worship the Father in spirit and truth. Yes, the Father wants such people to worship Him. God is Spirit, and those who worship Him must worship in spirit and truth.

John 4:23-24 HCSB

Worship the Lord with gladness. Come before him, singing with joy. Acknowledge that the Lord is God! He made us, and we are his. We are his people, the sheep of his pasture.

Psalm 100:2-3 NLT

More Ideas for Your Journey

Worship is about rekindling an ashen heart into a blazing fire.

Liz Curtis Higgs

Worship is God-centered, aware of one another only in that deep, joyous awareness of being caught up together in God.

Anne Ortlund

God asks that we worship Him with our concentrated minds as well as with our wills and emotions. A divided and scattered mind is not effective.

Catherine Marshall

A Mother's Prayer

Heavenly Father, let today and every day be a time of worship for me and my family. Let us worship You, not only with words, but also with deeds. In the quiet moments of the day, let us praise You and thank You for creating us, loving us, guiding us, and saving us. Amen

His Commandments

Follow the whole instruction the Lord your God has commanded you, so that you may live, prosper, and have a long life in the land you will possess.

Deuteronomy 5:33 HCSB

God gave us His commandments for a reason: so that we might obey them and be blessed. Elisabeth Elliot advised, "Obedience to God is our job. The results of that obedience are God's." These words should serve to remind us that obedience is imperative. But, we live in a world that presents us with countless temptations to disobey God's laws.

When we stray from God's path, we suffer. So, whenever we are confronted with sin, we have clear instructions: we must walk—or better yet run—in the opposite direction.

More from God's Word

He who has My commandments and keeps them, it is he who loves Me. And he who loves Me will be loved by My Father, and I will love him and manifest Myself to him.

John 14:21 NKJV

If only you had paid attention to My commands. Then your peace would have been like a river, and your righteousness like the waves of the sea.

Isaiah 48:18 HCSB

This is how we are sure that we have come to know Him: by keeping His commands.

1 John 2:3 HCSB

For this is the love of God, that we keep His commandments. And His commandments are not burdensome.

1 John 5:3 NKJV

Be still, and know that I am God . . . .

Psalm 46:10 KJV

More Ideas for Your Journey

The Ten Commandments were given to evoke fear and reverence for the Holy One so that obedience and blessing might result.

Beth Moore

Don't worry about what you do not understand. Worry about what you do understand in the Bible but do not live by.

Corrie ten Boom

Only grief and disappointment can result from continued violation of the divine principles that underlie the spiritual life.

A. W. Tozer

A Mother's Prayer

Thank You, Dear Lord, for loving me enough to give me rules to live by. Let me live by Your commandments, and let me lead others to do the same. Let me walk righteously in Your way, Dear Lord, this day and every day. Amen

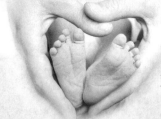

Media Messages

Set your minds on what is above, not on what is on the earth.

Colossians 3:2 HCSB

Sometimes it's hard being a woman of faith, especially when the world keeps pumping out messages that are contrary to your beliefs.

Beware! The media is working around the clock in an attempt to rearrange your priorities. The media says that appearance is all-important, that thinness is all-important, and that social standing is all-important. But guess what? Those messages are untrue. The important things in life have little to do with appearances. The all-important things in life have to do with your faith, your family, and your future. Period.

Because you live in the 21st century, you are relentlessly bombarded by media messages that are contrary to your faith. Take those messages with a grain of salt—or better yet, don't take them at all.

More Ideas for Your Journey

As we have by faith said no to sin, so we should by faith say yes to God and set our minds on things above, where Christ is seated in the heavenlies.

Vonette Bright

The more we stuff ourselves with material pleasures, the less we seem to appreciate life.

Barbara Johnson

Our fight is not against any physical enemy; it is against organizations and powers that are spiritual. We must struggle against sin all our lives, but we are assured we will win.

Corrie ten Boom

A Mother's Prayer

Lord, this world is a crazy place, and I have many opportunities to stray from Your commandments. Help me turn to obey You! Let me keep Christ in my heart, and let me put the devil in his place: far away from me! Amen

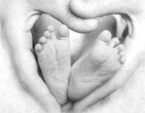

Time for Praising God

Therefore, through Him let us continually offer up to God a sacrifice of praise, that is, the fruit of our lips that confess His name.

Hebrews 13:15 HCSB

God has given you treasures that are beyond measure. He sent His only begotten Son to die for you, and He gave you a family to care for and to love. God has given you another day of life, and He has filled it to the brim with opportunities to celebrate and to serve. What should you do in return for God's priceless gifts? You should praise Him always.

Today, as you travel to work, as you hug your child or kiss your husband, as you gaze upon a passing cloud or marvel at a glorious sunset, think of what God has done for you, for yours, and for all of us. And, every time you notice a gift from the Giver of all things good, praise Him. His works are marvelous, His gifts are beyond understanding, and His love endures forever.

More from God's Word

Praise the Lord, all nations! Glorify Him, all peoples! For great is His faithful love to us; the Lord's faithfulness endures forever. Hallelujah!

Psalm 117 HCSB

But I will hope continually and will praise You more and more.

Psalm 71:14 HCSB

So that at the name of Jesus every knee should bow—of those who are in heaven and on earth and under the earth—and every tongue should confess that Jesus Christ is Lord, to the glory of God the Father.

Philippians 2:10-11 HCSB

Enter into his gates with thanksgiving, and into his courts with praise: be thankful unto him, and bless his name. For the LORD is good; his mercy is everlasting; and his truth endureth to all generations.

Psalm 100:4-5 KJV

In everything give thanks; for this is the will of God in Christ Jesus for you.

2 Thessalonians 5:18 NKJV

More Ideas for Your Journey

Two wings are necessary to lift our souls toward God: prayer and praise. Prayer asks. Praise accepts the answer.

Mrs. Charles E. Cowman

Nothing we do is more powerful or more life-changing than praising God.

Stormie Omartian

When we come before the Lord with praise, humbly repent of our transgressions, and in obedience present our petitions to God according to the guidelines set out for us in Scripture, He will answer.

Shirley Dobson

A Mother's Prayer

Dear Lord, today and every day we will praise You. We will come to You with hope in our hearts and words of gratitude on our lips. Let our thoughts, our prayers, our words, and our deeds praise You now and forever. Amen

Every Day with God

Morning by morning he wakens me and opens my understanding to his will. The Sovereign Lord has spoken to me, and I have listened.

Isaiah 50:4-5 NLT

Each new day is a gift from God, and wise moms spend a few quiet moments each morning thanking the Giver. Daily life is woven together with the threads of habit, and no habit is more important to our spiritual health than the discipline of daily prayer and devotion to the Creator.

When we begin each day with our heads bowed and our hearts lifted, we remind ourselves of God's love, His protection, and His commandments. And if we are wise, we align our priorities for the coming day with the teachings and commandments that God has given us through His Holy Word.

Are you seeking to change some aspect of your life? Then take time out of your hectic schedule to spend time each day with your Creator. Do you seek to improve the condition of your spiritual or physical health? If so, ask for God's help and ask for it many times each day . . . starting with your morning devotional.

More from God's Word

Teach me Your way, Lord, and I will live by Your truth. Give me an undivided mind to fear Your name.

Psalm 86:11 HCSB

I will instruct you and show you the way to go; with My eye on you, I will give counsel.

Psalm 32:8 HCSB

Happy is the man who finds wisdom, and the man who gains understanding.

Proverbs 3:13 NKJV

But grow in the grace and knowledge of our Lord and Savior Jesus Christ. To Him be the glory both now and to the day of eternity.

2 Peter 3:18 HCSB

In all your ways acknowledge Him, and He shall direct your paths.

Proverbs 3:6 NKJV

More Ideas for Your Journey

God is a place of safety you can run to, but it helps if you are running to Him on a daily basis so that you are in familiar territory.

Stormie Omartian

How motivating it has been for me to view my early morning devotions as time of retreat alone with Jesus, Who desires that I "come with Him by myself to a quiet place" in order to pray, read His Word, listen for His voice, and be renewed in my spirit.

Anne Graham Lotz

If you, too, will learn to wait upon God, to get alone with Him, and remain silent so that you can hear His voice when He is ready to speak to you, what a difference it will make in your life!

Kay Arthur

A Mother's Prayer

Lord, help me to hear Your direction for my life in the quiet moments when I study Your Holy Word. And as I go about my daily activities, let everything that I say and do be pleasing to You. Amen

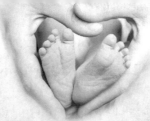

Too Busy to Pray?

The intense prayer of the righteous is very powerful.

James 5:16 HCSB

Does your family pray together often, or just at church? Are you a little band of prayer warriors, or have you retreated from God's battlefield? Do you and yours pray only at mealtimes, or do you pray much more often than that? The answer to these questions will determine, to a surprising extent, the level of your family's spiritual health.

Jesus made it clear to His disciples: they should pray always. And so should you. Genuine, heartfelt prayer changes things and it changes you. When you lift your heart to the Father, you open yourself to a never-ending source of divine wisdom and infinite love.

Your family's prayers are powerful. So, as you go about your daily activities, remember God's instructions: "Rejoice always! Pray constantly. Give thanks in everything, for this is God's will for you in Christ Jesus" (1 Thessalonians 5:16-18 HCSB). Start praying in the morning and keep praying until you fall off to sleep at night. And rest assured: God is always listening, and He always wants to hear from you and your family.

More from God's Word

Let the words of my mouth and the meditation of my heart be acceptable in Your sight, O Lord, my strength and my Redeemer.

Psalm 19:14 NKJV

Don't worry about anything, but in everything, through prayer and petition with thanksgiving, let your requests be made known to God.

Philippians 4:6 HCSB

Rejoice in hope; be patient in affliction; be persistent in prayer.

Romans 12:12 HCSB

Ask, and it shall be given you; seek, and ye shall find; knock, and it shall be opened unto you: for every one that asketh receiveth; and he that seeketh findeth; and to him that knocketh it shall be opened.

Matthew 7:7-8 KJV

More Ideas for Your Journey

When there is a matter that requires definite prayer, pray until you believe God and until you can thank Him for His answer.

Hannah Whitall Smith

As we join together in prayer, we draw on God's enabling might in a way that multiplies our own efforts many times over.

Shirley Dobson

When you ask God to do something, don't ask timidly; put your whole heart into it.

Marie T. Freeman

A Mother's Prayer

Lord, make me a prayerful Christian. In good times and in bad times, in whatever state I find myself, let me turn my prayers to You. You always hear my prayers, God; let me always pray them! Amen

Celebrate!

Rejoice in the Lord always. I will say it again: Rejoice!

Philippians 4:4 HCSB

Are you a mom who celebrates life? Hopefully you are! God has richly blessed you, and He wants you to rejoice in His gifts.

God fills each day to the brim with possibilities, and He challenges each of us to use our gifts for the glory of His kingdom. When we honor the Father and place Him at the center of our lives, every day becomes a cause for celebration.

Today is a non-renewable resource—once it's gone, it's gone forever. Our responsibility—both as mothers and as believers—is to use this day in the service of God's will and in the service of His people. When we do so, we enrich our own lives and the lives of those whom we love. And the Father smiles.

More from God's Word

This is the day the LORD has made; we will rejoice and be glad in it.

Psalm 118:24 NKJV

Delight yourself also in the Lord, and He shall give you the desires of your heart.

Psalm 37:4 NKJV

If they serve Him obediently, they will end their days in prosperity and their years in happiness.

Job 36:11 HCSB

The one who understands a matter finds success, and the one who trusts in the Lord will be happy.

Proverbs 16:20 HCSB

Rejoice in the Lord, you righteous ones; praise from the upright is beautiful.

Psalm 33:1 HCSB

More Ideas for Your Journey

Our sense of joy, satisfaction, and fulfillment in life increases, no matter what the circumstances, if we are in the center of God's will.

Billy Graham

If you can forgive the person you were, accept the person you are, and believe in the person you will become, you are headed for joy. So celebrate your life.

Barbara Johnson

Unparalleled joy and victory come from allowing Christ to do "the hard thing" with us.

Beth Moore

A Mother's Prayer

Dear Lord, today, I will join in the celebration of life. I will be a joyful Christian, and I will share my joy with all those who cross my path. You have given me countless blessings, Lord, and today I will thank You by celebrating my life, my faith, and my Savior. Amen

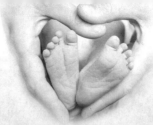

You'd Better Beware

Do not be conquered by evil, but conquer evil with good.

Romans 12:21 HCSB

This world is God's creation, and it contains the wonderful fruits of His handiwork. But, it also contains countless opportunities to stray from God's will. Temptations are everywhere, and the devil, it seems, never takes a day off. Our task, as caring mothers, is to do all that we can to protect our families from the evils of the world.

We must recognize evil and fight it. When we observe life objectively, and when we do so with eyes and hearts that are attuned to God's Holy Word, we can no longer be neutral believers. And when we are no longer neutral, God rejoices while the devil despairs.

More from God's Word

Therefore, submit to God. But resist the Devil, and he will flee from you. Draw near to God, and He will draw near to you. Cleanse your hands, sinners, and purify your hearts, double-minded people!

James 4:7-8 HCSB

For everyone who practices wicked things hates the light and avoids it, so that his deeds may not be exposed. But anyone who lives by the truth comes to the light, so that his works may be shown to be accomplished by God.

John 3:20–21 HCSB

Don't consider yourself to be wise; fear the Lord and turn away from evil.

Proverbs 3:7 HCSB

But the path of the just is like the shining sun, that shines ever brighter unto the perfect day. The way of the wicked is like darkness; they do not know what makes them stumble.

Proverbs 4:18-19 NKJV

Be sober! Be on the alert! Your adversary the Devil is prowling around like a roaring lion, looking for anyone he can devour.

1 Peter 5:8 HCSB

More Ideas for Your Journey

We are in a continual battle with the spiritual forces of evil, but we will triumph when we yield to God's leading and call on His powerful presence in prayer.

Shirley Dobson

Light is stronger than darkness—darkness cannot "comprehend" or "overcome" it.

Anne Graham Lotz

Where God's ministers are most successful, there the powers of darkness marshal their forces for the conflict.

Lottie Moon

A Mother's Prayer

Lord, strengthen my walk with You. Evil comes in many disguises, and sometimes it is only with Your help that I can recognize right from wrong. Your presence in my life enables me to choose truth and to live a life pleasing to You. May I always live in Your presence. Amen

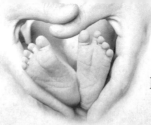

Studying the Word

For I am not ashamed of the gospel, because it is God's power for salvation to everyone who believes.

Romans 1:16 HCSB

God's Word is unlike any other book. The Bible is a roadmap for life here on earth and for life eternal. As Christians, we are called upon to study God's Holy Word, to trust His Word, to follow its commandments, and to share its Good News with the world.

The words of Matthew 4:4 remind us that, "Man shall not live by bread alone but by every word that proceedeth out of the mouth of God" (KJV). As believers, we must study the Bible and meditate upon its meaning for our lives. Otherwise, we deprive ourselves of a priceless gift from our Creator.

Warren Wiersbe observed, "When the child of God looks into the Word of God, he sees the Son of God. And, he is transformed by the Spirit of God to share in the glory of God." God's Holy Word is, indeed, a transforming, life-changing, one-of-a-kind treasure. And, a passing acquaintance with the Good Book is insufficient for Christians who seek to obey God's Word and to understand His will. After all, man—and moms—do not live by bread alone . . .

More from God's Word

All Scripture is inspired by God and is profitable for teaching, for rebuking, for correcting, for training in righteousness, so that the man of God may be complete, equipped for every good work.

2 Timothy 3:16-17 HCSB

Man shall not live by bread alone, but by every word that proceeds from the mouth of God.

Matthew 4:4 NKJV

Your word is a lamp for my feet and a light on my path.

Psalm 119:105 HCSB

Heaven and earth will pass away, but My words will never pass away.

Matthew 24:35 HCSB

More Ideas for Your Journey

The Reference Point for the Christian is the Bible. All values, judgments, and attitudes must be gauged in relationship to this Reference Point.

Ruth Bell Graham

Study the Bible and observe how the persons behaved and how God dealt with them. There is explicit teaching on every condition of life.

Corrie ten Boom

The Bible is a remarkable commentary on perspective. Through its divine message, we are brought face to face with issues and tests in daily living and how, by the power of the Holy Spirit, we are enabled to respond positively to them.

Luci Swindoll

A Mother's Prayer

Dear Lord, the Bible is Your gift to me. Let me use it, let me trust it, and let me obey it, today and every day that I live. Amen

God Can Handle It

*For I, the Lord your God, hold your right hand and say to
you: Do not fear, I will help you.*

Isaiah 41:13 HCSB

It's a promise that is made over and over again in the
Bible: Whatever "it" is, God can handle it.

Life isn't always easy. Far from it! Sometimes,
life can be very, very tough. But even then, even during our darkest moments, we're protected by a loving
Heavenly Father. When we're worried, God can reas-
sure us; when we're sad, God can comfort us. When our
hearts are broken, God is not just near, He is here. So
we must lift our thoughts and prayers to Him. When we
do, He will answer our prayers. Why? Because He is our
Shepherd, and He has promised to protect us now and
forever.

More from God's Word

Now the God of all grace, who called you to His eternal glory in Christ Jesus, will personally restore, establish, strengthen, and support you.

1 Peter 5:10 HCSB

Peace, peace to you, and peace to your helpers! For your God helps you.

1 Chronicles 12:18 NKJV

The LORD is my strength and song, and He has become my salvation; He is my God, and I will praise Him . . .

Exodus 15:2 NKJV

Therefore whoever hears these sayings of Mine, and does them, I will liken him to a wise man who built his house on the rock: and the rain descended, the floods came, and the winds blew and beat on that house; and it did not fall, for it was founded on the rock.

Matthew 7:24-25 NKJV

He gives power to the weak, and to those who have no might He increases strength.

Isaiah 40:29 NKJV

More Ideas for Your Journey

God uses our most stumbling, faltering faith-steps as the open door to His doing for us "more than we ask or think."

Catherine Marshall

God is always sufficient in perfect proportion to our need.

Beth Moore

God's saints in all ages have realized that God was enough for them. God is enough for time; God is enough for eternity. God is enough!

Hannah Whitall Smith

A Mother's Prayer

Dear Lord, whatever "it" is, You can handle it! Let me turn to You when I am fearful or worried. You are my loving Heavenly Father, sufficient in all things and I will always trust You. Amen

Those Difficult Days

We are pressured in every way but not crushed; we are perplexed but not in despair.

2 Corinthians 4:8 HCSB

As every mother knows, some days are just plain difficult. Every mother faces days when the baby is sick, when the laundry is piled high, and the bills are piled even higher.

When we find ourselves overtaken by the inevitable frustrations of life, we must catch ourselves, take a deep breath, and lift our thoughts upward. Although we are here on earth struggling to rise above the distractions of the day, we need never struggle alone. God is here—eternal and faithful—and, if we reach out to Him, He will restore perspective and peace to our souls.

Sometimes even the most devout Christian moms can become discouraged, and you are no exception. After all, you live in a world where expectations can be high and demands can be even higher.

If you find yourself enduring difficult circumstances, remember that God remains in His heaven. If you become discouraged with the direction of your day or your life, take a moment to offer your thoughts and prayers to Him. He is a God of possibility, not negativity. He will guide you through your difficulties and beyond them.

More from God's Word

The Lord is a refuge for the oppressed, a refuge in times of trouble.

Psalm 9:9 HCSB

I will be with you when you pass through the waters . . . when you walk through the fire . . . the flame will not burn you. For I the Lord your God, the Holy One of Israel, and your Savior.

Isaiah 43:2-3 HCSB

When you are in distress and all these things have happened to you, you will return to the Lord your God in later days and obey Him. He will not leave you, destroy you, or forget the covenant with your fathers that He swore to them by oath, because the Lord your God is a compassionate God.

Deuteronomy 4:30-31 HCSB

More Ideas for Your Journey

When the hard times of life come, we know that no matter how tragic the circumstances seem, no matter how long the spiritual drought, no matter how long and dark the days, the sun is sure to break through; the dawn will come.

Gloria Gaither

When life is difficult, God wants us to have a faith that trusts and waits.

Kay Arthur

For whatever life holds for you and your family in the coming days, weave the unfailing fabric of God's Word through your heart and mind. It will hold strong, even if the rest of life unravels.

Gigi Graham Tchividjian

A Mother's Prayer

Dear Lord, when the day is difficult, give me perspective and faith. When I am weak, give me strength. Let me trust in Your promises, Father, and let me live with the assurance that You are with me not only today, but also throughout all eternity. Amen

Beyond Discouragement

But as for you, be strong; don't be discouraged, for your work has a reward.

2 Chronicles 15:7 HCSB

We Christians have many reasons to celebrate. God is in His heaven; Christ has risen, and we are the sheep of His flock. Yet sometimes, even the most devout Christian women can become discouraged. After all, we live in a world where expectations can be high and demands can be even higher. If you become discouraged with the direction of your day or your life, turn your thoughts and prayers to God. He is a God of possibility, not negativity. He will help you count your blessings instead of your hardships. And then, with a renewed spirit of optimism and hope, you can properly thank your Father in heaven for His blessings, for His love, and for His Son.

More from God's Word

We are hard pressed on every side, yet not crushed; we are perplexed, but not in despair.

2 Corinthians 4:8 NKJV

I called to the Lord in my distress; I called to my God. From His temple He heard my voice.

2 Samuel 22:7 HCSB

I will be with you when you pass through the waters . . . when you walk through the fire . . . the flame will not burn you. For I the Lord your God, the Holy One of Israel, and your Savior.

Isaiah 43:2-3 HCSB

Consider it a great joy, my brothers, whenever you experience various trials, knowing that the testing of your faith produces endurance. But endurance must do its complete work, so that you may be mature and complete, lacking nothing.

James 1:2-4 HCSB

These things I have spoken to you, that in Me you may have peace. In the world you will have tribulation; but be of good cheer, I have overcome the world.

John 16:33 NKJV

More Ideas for Your Journey

God does not dispense strength and encouragement like a druggist fills your prescription. The Lord doesn't promise to give us something to take so we can handle our weary moments. He promises us Himself. That is all. And that is enough.

Charles Swindoll

Overcoming discouragement is simply a matter of taking away the DIS and adding the EN.

Barbara Johnson

Working in the vineyard, / Working all the day, / Never be discouraged, / Only watch and pray.

Fanny Crosby

A Mother's Prayer

Heavenly Father, when I am discouraged, I will turn to You, and I will also turn to my Christian friends. I Thank You, Father, for friends and family members who are willing to encourage me. I will acknowledge their encouragement, and I will share it. Amen

The Gift of Eternal Life

For God so loved the world, that he gave his only begotten Son, that whosoever believeth in him should not perish, but have everlasting life.

John 3:16 KJV

Your life here on earth is merely a preparation for a far different life to come: the eternal life that God promises to those who welcome His Son into their hearts.

As a mere mortal, your vision for the future is finite. God's vision is not burdened by such limitations: His plans extend throughout all eternity. Thus, God's plans for you are not limited to the ups and downs of everyday life. Your Heavenly Father has bigger things in mind.

As you struggle with the occasional hardships and disappointments of life, remember that God has invited you to accept His abundance not only for today but for all eternity. So keep things in perspective. Although you will inevitably encounter defeats in this world, you'll have all eternity to celebrate the ultimate victory in the next.

More from God's Word

Jesus said to her, "I am the resurrection and the life. The one who believes in Me, even if he dies, will live. Everyone who lives and believes in Me will never die—ever. Do you believe this?"

John 11:25-26 HCSB

And this is the testimony: God has given us eternal life, and this life is in His Son. The one who has the Son has life. The one who doesn't have the Son of God does not have life. I have written these things to you who believe in the name of the Son of God, so that you may know that you have eternal life.

1 John 5:11-13 HCSB

We do not want you to be uninformed, brothers, concerning those who are asleep, so that you will not grieve like the rest, who have no hope. Since we believe that Jesus died and rose again, in the same way God will bring with Him those who have fallen asleep through Jesus.

1 Thessalonians 4:13-14 HCSB

More Ideas for Your Journey

If you are a believer, your judgment will not determine your eternal destiny. Christ's finished work on Calvary was applied to you the moment you accepted Christ as Savior.

Beth Moore

The gift of God is eternal life, spiritual life, abundant life through faith in Jesus Christ, the Living Word of God.

Anne Graham Lotz

I can still hardly believe it. I, with shriveled, bent fingers, atrophied muscles, gnarled knees, and no feeling from the shoulders down, will one day have a new body— light, bright and clothed in righteousness—powerful and dazzling.

Joni Eareckson Tada

A Mother's Prayer

Lord, You have given me the gift of eternal life through Christ Jesus. I praise You for that priceless gift. Because I am saved, I will share the story of Your Son and the glory of my salvation with a world that desperately needs Your grace. Amen

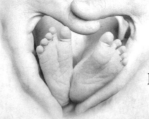

Forgiveness Now

All bitterness, anger and wrath, insult and slander must be removed from you, along with all wickedness. And be kind and compassionate to one another, forgiving one another, just as God also forgave you in Christ.

Ephesians 4:31-32 HCSB

Even the most mild-mannered moms will, on occasion, have reason to become angry with the inevitable shortcomings of family members and friends. But wise women are quick to forgive others, just as God has forgiven them.

Forgiveness is God's commandment, but oh how difficult a commandment it can be to follow. Being frail, fallible, imperfect human beings, we are quick to anger, quick to blame, slow to forgive, and even slower to forget. No matter. Even when forgiveness is difficult, God's Word is clear.

If, in your heart, you hold bitterness against even a single person, forgive. If there exists even one person, alive or dead, whom you have not forgiven, follow God's commandment and His will for your life: forgive. If you are embittered against yourself for some past mistake or shortcoming, forgive. Then, to the best of your abilities, forget, and move on. Bitterness and regret are not part of God's plan for your life. Forgiveness is.

More from God's Word

See to it that no one repays evil for evil to anyone, but always pursue what is good for one another and for all.

1 Thessalonians 5:15 HCSB

A person's insight gives him patience, and his virtue is to overlook an offense.

Proverbs 19:11 HCSB

And forgive us our sins, for we ourselves also forgive everyone in debt to us.

Luke 11:4 HCSB

And whenever you stand praying, if you have anything against anyone, forgive him, so that your Father in heaven may also forgive you your wrongdoing.

Mark 11:25 HCSB

More Ideas for Your Journey

Forgiveness is the precondition of love.

Catherine Marshall

God expects us to forgive others as He has forgiven us; we are to follow His example by having a forgiving heart.

Vonette Bright

I believe that forgiveness can become a continuing cycle: because God forgives us, we're to forgive others; because we forgive others, God forgives us. Scripture presents both parts of the cycle.

Shirley Dobson

A Mother's Prayer

Lord, I know that I need to forgive others just as You have forgiven me. Help me to be an example of forgiveness to my children. Keep me mindful, Father, that I am never fully liberated until I have been freed from the chains of bitterness—and that You offer me that freedom through Your Son, Christ Jesus. Amen

Fitness Matters

Whatever you eat or drink or whatever you do, you must do all for the glory of God.

1 Corinthians 10:31 NLT

Are you shaping up or spreading out? Do you eat sensibly and exercise regularly, or do you spend most of your time on the couch with a high-calorie snack in one hand and a clicker in the other? Are you choosing to treat your body like a temple or a trash heap? How you answer these questions will help determine how long you live and how well you live.

Physical fitness is a choice, a choice that requires discipline—it's as simple as that. So, do yourself this favor: treat your body like a one-of-a-kind gift from God . . . because that's precisely what your body is.

More Ideas for Your Journey

God wants you to give Him your body. Some people do foolish things with their bodies. God wants your body as a holy sacrifice.

Warren Wiersbe

Our primary motivation should not be for more energy or to avoid a heart attack but to please God with our bodies.

Carole Lewis

People are funny. When they are young, they will spend their health to get wealth. Later, they will gladly pay all they have trying to get their health back.

John Maxwell

A Mother's Prayer

Lord, all that I am belongs to You. As I serve You with all that I am and all that I have, help me to honor You by caring for the body that You have given me. Amen.

Your Noisy World

Be silent before the Lord and wait expectantly for Him.

Psalm 37:7 HCSB

Face it: We live in a noisy world, a world filled with distractions, frustrations, and complications. But if we allow those distractions to separate us from God's peace, we do ourselves a profound disservice.

Are you one of those busy moms who rushes through the day with scarcely a single moment for quiet contemplation and prayer? If so, it's time to reorder your priorities.

Nothing is more important than the time you spend with your Savior. So be still and claim the inner peace that is your spiritual birthright: the peace of Jesus Christ. It is offered freely; it has been paid for in full; it is yours for the asking. So ask. And then share.

More from God's Word

In quietness and confidence shall be your strength.

Isaiah 30:15 NKJV

The one who is from God listens to God's words. This is why you don't listen, because you are not from God.

John 8:47 HCSB

What's this? Fools out shopping for wisdom! They wouldn't recognize it if they saw it!

Proverbs 17:16 MSG

I wait quietly before God, for my hope is in him.

Psalm 62:5 NLT

Be still, and know that I am God.

Psalm 46:10 NKJV

More Ideas for Your Journey

Jesus taught us by example to get out of the rat race and recharge our batteries.

Barbara Johnson

The manifold rewards of a serious, consistent prayer life demonstrate clearly that time with our Lord should be our first priority.

Shirley Dobson

The Lord Jesus, available to people much of the time, left them, sometimes a great while before day, to go up to the hills where He could commune in solitude with His Father.

Elisabeth Elliot

A Mother's Prayer

Lord, Your Holy Word is a light unto the world; let me study it, trust it, and share it with all who cross my path. Let me discover You, Father, in the quiet moments of the day. And, in all that I say and do, help me to be a worthy witness as I share the Good News of Your perfect Son and Your perfect Word. Amen

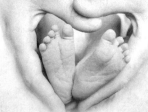

When Mistakes Are Made

Therefore, if anyone is in Christ, he is a new creation; the old has gone, the new has come!

2 Corinthians 5:17 NIV

As parents, we are far from perfect. And, without question, our children are imperfect as well. Thus, we are imperfect parents raising imperfect children, and, as a result, mistakes are bound to happen.

Has someone in your family experienced a recent setback? If so, it's time to start looking for the lesson that God is trying to teach. It's time to learn what needs to be learned, change what needs to be changed, and move on.

You and your loved ones should view mistakes as opportunities to reassess God's will for your lives. And while you're at it, you should consider life's inevitable disappointments to be powerful opportunities to learn more—more about yourselves, more about your circumstances, and more about your world.

More Ideas for Your Journey

Father, take our mistakes and turn them into opportunities.

Max Lucado

God is able to take mistakes, when they are committed to Him, and make of them something for our good and for His glory.

Ruth Bell Graham

If at first you don't succeed, read the Instruction Manual—God's.

Anonymous

A Mother's Prayer

Lord, sometimes I make mistakes and fall short of Your commandments. When I do, forgive me, Father. And help me learn from my mistakes so that I can be a better servant to You and a better example to my family and friends. Amen

Real Wisdom

Acquire wisdom—how much better it is than gold! And acquire understanding—it is preferable to silver.

Proverbs 16:16 HCSB

Do you seek wisdom for yourself and for your family? Of course you do. But as a savvy mom, you know that wisdom can be an elusive commodity in today's troubled world. In a society filled with temptations and distractions; it's easy for parents and children alike to stray far from the source of the ultimate wisdom: God's Holy Word.

When you begin a daily study of God's Word and live according to His commandments, you will become wise . . . in time. But don't expect to open your Bible today and be wise tomorrow. Wisdom is not like a mushroom; it does not spring up overnight. It is, instead, like an oak tree that starts as a tiny acorn, grows into a sapling, and eventually reaches up to the sky, tall and strong.

Today and every day, study God's Word and live by it. In time, you will accumulate a storehouse of wisdom that will enrich your own life and the lives of your family members, your friends, and the world.

More from God's Word

The fear of the Lord is the beginning of wisdom; a good understanding have all those who do His commandments. His praise endures forever.

Psalm 111:10 NKJV

Therefore, everyone who hears these words of Mine and acts on them will be like a sensible man who built his house on the rock. The rain fell, the rivers rose, and the winds blew and pounded that house. Yet it didn't collapse, because its foundation was on the rock.

Matthew 7:24–25 HCSB

A wise man will hear and increase learning, and a man of understanding will attain wise counsel.

Proverbs 1:5 NKJV

Teach me, O Lord, the way of Your statutes, and I shall keep it to the end.

Psalm 119:33 NKJV

More Ideas for Your Journey

When you and I are related to Jesus Christ, our strength and wisdom and peace and joy and love and hope may run out, but His life rushes in to keep us filled to the brim. We are showered with blessings, not because of anything we have or have not done, but simply because of Him.

Anne Graham Lotz

No matter how many books you read, no matter how many schools you attend, you're never really wise until you start making wise choices.

Marie T. Freeman

Wisdom is knowledge applied. Head knowledge is useless on the battlefield. Knowledge stamped on the heart makes one wise.

Beth Moore

A Mother's Prayer

Dear Lord, give me wisdom to love my family, to care for them, to teach them, and to lead them. Make me wise in Your ways and in Your Holy Word. Let me share Your wisdom through words and deeds, today and every day that I live. Amen

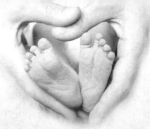

The Hem of His Garment

Now faith is being sure of what we hope for and certain of what we do not see.

Hebrews 11:1 NIV

A suffering woman sought healing in an unusual way: she simply touched the hem of Jesus' garment. When she did, Jesus turned and said, "Daughter, be of good comfort; thy faith hath made thee whole" (Matthew 9:22 KJV). We, too, can be made whole when we place our faith completely and unwaveringly in the person of Jesus Christ.

Concentration camp survivor Corrie ten Boom relied on faith during ten months of imprisonment and torture. Later, despite the fact that four of her family members had died in Nazi death camps, Corrie's faith was unshaken. She wrote, "There is no pit so deep that God's love is not deeper still." Christians take note: Genuine faith in God means faith in all circumstances, happy or sad, joyful or tragic.

When you place your faith, your trust, indeed your life in the hands of Christ Jesus, you'll be amazed at the marvelous things He can do with you and through you. So strengthen your faith through praise, through worship, through Bible study, and through prayer. Then, trust God's plans. Your Heavenly Father is standing at the door of your heart. If you reach out to Him in faith, He will give you peace and heal your broken spirit. Be content to touch even the smallest fragment of the Master's garment, and He will make you whole.

More from God's Word

If you do not stand firm in your faith, then you will not stand at all.

Isaiah 7:9 HCSB

Be alert, stand firm in the faith, be brave and strong.

1 Corinthians 16:13 HCSB

For we walk by faith, not by sight.

2 Corinthians 5:7 HCSB

Now faith is the reality of what is hoped for, the proof of what is not seen.

Hebrews 11:1 HCSB

More Ideas for Your Journey

Faith does not concern itself with the entire journey. One step is enough.

Mrs. Charles E. Cowman

Just as our faith strengthens our prayer life, so do our prayers deepen our faith. Let us pray often, starting today, for a deeper, more powerful faith.

Shirley Dobson

If God chooses to remain silent, faith is content.

Ruth Bell Graham

A Mother's Prayer

Lord, help me to be a mother whose faith is evident to my family and friends. Help me to remember that You are always near and that You can overcome any challenge. With Your love and Your power, Lord, I will live courageously and share my faith with others, today and every day. Amen

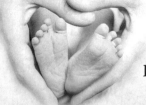

To Shop or Not to Shop?

Don't collect for yourselves treasures on earth, where moth and rust destroy and where thieves break in and steal. But collect for yourselves treasures in heaven, where neither moth nor rust destroys, and where thieves don't break in and steal. For where your treasure is, there your heart will be also.

Matthew 6:19-21 HCSB

In the demanding world in which we live, financial prosperity can be a good thing, but spiritual prosperity is profoundly more important. Yet our society leads us to believe otherwise. The world glorifies material possessions, personal fame, and physical beauty above all else; these things, of course, are totally unimportant to God. God sees the human heart, and that's what is important to Him.

As you prioritize your day, remember this: The world will do everything it can to convince you that "things" are important. The world will tempt you to value fortune above faith and possessions above peace. God, on the other hand, will try to convince you that your relationship with Him is all-important. Trust God.

More from God's Word

And He told them, "Watch out and be on guard against all greed, because one's life is not in the abundance of his possessions."

Luke 12:15 HCSB

For what does it benefit a man to gain the whole world yet lose his life? What can a man give in exchange for his life?

Mark 8:36-37 HCSB

Anyone trusting in his riches will fall, but the righteous will flourish like foliage.

Proverbs 11:28 HCSB

For the mind-set of the flesh is death, but the mind-set of the Spirit is life and peace.

Romans 8:6 HCSB

If your wealth increases, don't make it the center of your life.

Psalm 62:10 NLT

More Ideas for Your Journey

We own too many things that aren't worth owning.

Marie T. Freeman

It's sobering to contemplate how much time, effort, sacrifice, compromise, and attention we give to acquiring and increasing our supply of something that is totally insignificant in eternity.

Anne Graham Lotz

As faithful stewards of what we have, ought we not to give earnest thought to our staggering surplus?

Elisabeth Elliot

A Mother's Prayer

Dear Lord, keep me mindful that material possession cannot bring me joy—my joy comes from You. I will share that joy with family, with friends, and with neighbors, this day and every day. Amen

Time: A Gift from God

So teach us to number our days, that we may gain a heart of wisdom.

Psalm 90:12 NKJV

As every mother knows all too well, there simply isn't enough time to do everything we want—and need—to do. That's why, as mothers, we should be so very careful about the ways that we choose to spend the time that God has given us.

Time is a nonrenewable gift from the Creator. But sometimes, we treat our time here on earth as if it were not a gift at all: We may be tempted to invest our lives in petty diversions or in trivial pursuits. But our Father in heaven beckons each of us to a higher calling.

An important element of our stewardship to God is the way that we choose to spend the time He has entrusted to us. Each waking moment holds the potential to do a good deed, to say a kind word, or to offer a heartfelt prayer. Our challenge, as believers, is to use our time wisely in the service of God's work and in accordance with His plan for our lives.

Each day is a special treasure to be savored and celebrated. May we—as Christian moms who have so much to celebrate—never fail to praise our Creator by rejoicing in this glorious day, and by using it wisely.

More Ideas for Your Journey

As we surrender the use of our time to the lordship of Christ, He will lead us to use it in the most productive way imaginable.

Charles Stanley

Overcommitment and time pressures are the greatest destroyers of marriages and families. It takes time to develop any friendship, whether with a loved one or with God himself.

James Dobson

A Mother's Prayer

Dear Lord, You have given me a wonderful gift: time here on earth. Let me use it wisely—for the glory of Your kingdom and the betterment of my family—today and every day that I live. Amen

Choosing to Be Kind

Just as you want others to do for you, do the same for them.

Luke 6:31 HCSB

Kindness is a choice. Sometimes, when we feel happy or generous, we find it easy to be kind. Other times, when we are discouraged or tired, we can scarcely summon the energy to utter a single kind word. But, God's commandment is clear: He intends that we make the conscious choice to treat others with kindness and respect, no matter our circumstances, no matter our emotions.

In the busyness and confusion of daily life, it is easy to lose focus, and it is easy to become frustrated. We are imperfect human beings struggling to manage our lives as best we can, but we often fall short. When we are distracted or disappointed, we may neglect to share a kind word or a kind deed. This oversight hurts others, but it hurts us most of all.

Today, slow yourself down and be alert for people who need your smile, your kind words, or your helping hand. Make kindness a centerpiece of your dealings with others. They will be blessed, and you will be too.

More from God's Word

Finally, all of you be of one mind, having compassion for one another; love as brothers, be tenderhearted, be courteous.

1 Peter 3:8 NKJV

Love is patient; love is kind.

1 Corinthians 13:4 HCSB

And may the Lord make you increase and abound in love to one another and to all.

1 Thessalonians 3:12 NKJV

And be kind and compassionate to one another, forgiving one another, just as God also forgave you in Christ.

Ephesians 4:32 HCSB

Pure and undefiled religion before our God and Father is this: to look after orphans and widows in their distress and to keep oneself unstained by the world.

James 1:27 HCSB

More Ideas for Your Journey

If we have the true love of God in our hearts, we will show it in our lives. We will not have to go up and down the earth proclaiming it. We will show it in everything we say or do.

D. L. Moody

Kindness in this world will do much to help others, not only to come into the light, but also to grow in grace day by day.

Fanny Crosby

Sometimes one little spark of kindness is all it takes to reignite the light of hope in a heart that's blinded by pain.

Barbara Johnson

A Mother's Prayer

Lord, make me a loving, encouraging Christian mother. And, let my love for Christ be reflected through the kindness that I show to those who need the healing touch of the Master's hand. Amen

Enthused About Life

Whatever you do, do it enthusiastically, as something done for the Lord and not for men.

Colossians 3:23 HCSB

D o you see each day as a glorious opportunity to serve God and to do His will? Are you enthused about life, or do you struggle through each day giving scarcely a thought to God's blessings?

If you're a mother with too many demands and too few hours in which to meet them, you are not alone. Motherhood is perhaps the world's most demanding profession. But don't fret. Instead, focus upon God and upon His love for you. Then, ask Him for the strength you need to fulfill your responsibilities. God will give you the energy to do the most important things on to-day's to-do list…if you ask Him. So ask Him.

More from God's Word

Never be lazy in your work, but serve the Lord enthusiastically.

Romans 12:11 NLT

Whatever work you do, do your best, because you are going to the grave, where there is no working . . . .

Ecclesiastes 9:10 NCV

I have seen that there is nothing better than for a person to enjoy his activities, because that is his reward. For who can enable him to see what will happen after he dies?

Ecclesiastes 3:22 HCSB

Do your work with enthusiasm. Work as if you were serving the Lord, not as if you were serving only men and women.

Ephesians 6:7 NCV

But those who wait on the LORD shall renew their strength; they shall mount up with wings like eagles, they shall run and not be weary, they shall walk and not faint.

Isaiah 40:31 NKJV

More Ideas for Your Journey

Catch on fire with enthusiasm and people will come for miles to watch you burn.

John Wesley

Enthusiasm, like the flu, is contagious—we get it from one another.

Barbara Johnson

One of the great needs in the church today is for every Christian to become enthusiastic about his faith in Jesus Christ.

Billy Graham

A Mother's Prayer

Dear Lord, let me be an enthusiastic participant in life. And let my enthusiasm bring honor and glory to You. Amen

Powerful Perseverance

For you need endurance, so that after you have done God's will, you may receive what was promised.

Hebrews 10:36 HCSB

Someone once said, "Life is a marathon, not a sprint." The same can be said for motherhood. Motherhood requires courage, perseverance, determination, and, of course, an unending supply of motherly love. Are you tired? Ask God for strength. Are you discouraged? Believe in His promises. Are you frustrated or fearful? Pray as if everything depended upon God, and work as if everything depended upon you. With God's help, you will find the strength to be the kind of mom who makes her Heavenly Father beam with pride.

More from God's Word

Do you not know that the runners in a stadium all race, but only one receives the prize? Run in such a way that you may win. Now everyone who competes exercises self-control in everything. However, they do it to receive a perishable crown, but we an imperishable one.

1 Corinthians 9:24-25 HCSB

But as for you, be strong; don't be discouraged, for your work has a reward.

2 Chronicles 15:7 HCSB

I have fought the good fight, I have finished the race, I have kept the faith.

2 Timothy 4:7 HCSB

So we must not get tired of doing good, for we will reap at the proper time if we don't give up.

Galatians 6:9 HCSB

Let us lay aside every weight and the sin that so easily ensnares us, and run with endurance the race that lies before us, keeping our eyes on Jesus, the source and perfecter of our faith.

Hebrews 12:1-2 HCSB

More Ideas for Your Journey

When you fall and skin your knees and skin your heart, He'll pick you up.

Charles Stanley

Your life is not a boring stretch of highway. It's a straight line to heaven. And just look at the fields ripening along the way. Look at the tenacity and endurance. Look at the grains of righteousness. You'll have quite a crop at harvest . . . so don't give up!

Joni Eareckson Tada

Failure is one of life's most powerful teachers. How we handle our failures determines whether we're going to simply "get by" in life or "press on."

Beth Moore

A Mother's Prayer

Dear Lord, when my responsibilities as a mother seem overwhelming, slow me down and give me perspective. Keep me steady and sure. When I become weary, let me persevere so that, in Your time, I might finish my work here on earth, and that You might then say, "Well done my good and faithful servant." Amen

The Best Policy

The honest person will live in safety, but the dishonest will be caught.

Proverbs 10:9 NCV

It has been said on many occasions and in many ways that honesty is the best policy. For believers, it is far more important to note that honesty is God's policy. And if we are to be servants worthy of Jesus Christ, we must be honest and forthright in our communications with others. Sometimes, honesty is difficult; sometimes, honesty is painful; sometimes, honesty is inconvenient; but always honesty is God's commandment.

In the Book of Proverbs, we read, "The Lord detests lying lips, but he delights in men who are truthful" (12:22 NIV). Clearly, we must strive to be men whose words are pleasing to our Creator. Truth is God's way, and it must be our way, too, even when telling the truth is difficult. As loving mothers, we can do no less.

More Ideas for Your Journey

Integrity is not a given factor in everyone's life. It is a result of self-discipline, inner trust, and a decision to be relentlessly honest in all situations in our lives.

John Maxwell

The single most important element in any human relationship is honesty—with oneself, with God, and with others.

Catherine Marshall

Much guilt arises in the life of the believer from practicing the chameleon life of environmental adaptation.

Beth Moore

A Mother's Prayer

Dear Lord, You command Your children to walk in truth. Let me follow Your commandment. Give me the courage to speak honestly, and let me walk righteously with You so that others might see Your eternal truth reflected in my words and my deeds. Amen

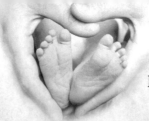

Saying "Thank You"

Give thanks to the Lord, for He is good; His faithful love endures forever.

Psalm 118:29 HCSB

As believing Christians, we are blessed beyond measure. God sent His only Son to die for our sins. And, God has given us the priceless gifts of eternal love and eternal life. We, in turn, are instructed to approach our Heavenly Father with reverence and thanksgiving. But, as busy mothers caught up in the inevitable demands of everyday life, we sometimes fail to pause and thank our Creator for the countless blessings He has bestowed upon us.

When we slow down and express our gratitude to the One who made us, we enrich our own lives and the lives of our loved ones. Thanksgiving should become a habit, a regular part of our daily routines. Yes, God has blessed us beyond measure, and we owe Him everything, including our eternal praise.

More from God's Word

In everything give thanks; for this is the will of God in Christ Jesus for you.

1 Thessalonians 5:18 NKJV

Thanks be to God for His indescribable gift.

2 Corinthians 9:15 HCSB

And let the peace of the Messiah, to which you were also called in one body, control your hearts. Be thankful.

Colossians 3:15 HCSB

It is good to give thanks to the Lord, and to sing praises to Your name, O Most High.

Psalm 92:1 NKJV

Enter into His gates with thanksgiving, and into His courts with praise. Be thankful to Him, and bless His name. For the Lord is good; His mercy is everlasting, and His truth endures to all generations.

Psalm 100:4-5 NKJV

More Ideas for Your Journey

God is in control, and therefore in everything I can give thanks, not because of the situation, but because of the One who directs and rules over it.

Kay Arthur

It is always possible to be thankful for what is given rather than to complain about what is not given. One or the other becomes a habit of life.

Elisabeth Elliot

Do you know that if at birth I had been able to make one petition, it would have been that I should be born blind? Because, when I get to heaven, the first face that shall ever gladden my sight will be that of my Savior!

Fanny Crosby

A Mother's Prayer

Dear Lord, You have blessed me with a loving family—make me a mother who is thankful, loving, responsible, and wise. I praise You, Father, for the gift of Your Son and for the gift of salvation. Let me be a joyful Christian and a worthy example, this day and every day that I live. Amen

The Wisdom Not to Judge

Do not judge, and you will not be judged. Do not condemn, and you will not be condemned. Forgive, and you will be forgiven.

Luke 6:37 HCSB

The warning of Matthew 7:1 is clear and simple: "Do not judge." Yet even the most devoted Christians may fall prey to a powerful yet subtle temptation: the temptation to judge others. But as obedient followers of Christ, we are commanded to refrain from such behavior.

As Jesus came upon a young woman who had been condemned by the Pharisees, He spoke not only to the crowd that was gathered there, but also to all generations when He warned, "He that is without sin among you, let him first cast a stone at her" (John 8:7 KJV). Christ's message is clear, and it applies not only to the Pharisees of ancient times, but also to us.

More from God's Word

Speak and act as those who will be judged by the law of freedom. For judgment is without mercy to the one who hasn't shown mercy. Mercy triumphs over judgment.

James 2:12-13 HCSB

When Jesus stood up, He said to her, "Woman, where are they? Has no one condemned you?" "No one, Lord," she answered. "Neither do I condemn you," said Jesus. "Go, and from now on do not sin any more."

John 8:10-11 HCSB

How can you say to your brother, "Brother, let me take out the speck that is in your eye," when you yourself don't see the log in your eye? Hypocrite! First take the log out of your eye, and then you will see clearly to take out the speck in your brother's eye.

Luke 6:42 HCSB

Therefore judge nothing before the time, until the Lord comes, who will both bring to light the hidden things of darkness and reveal the counsels of the hearts. Then each one's praise will come from God.

1 Corinthians 4:5 NKJV

More Ideas for Your Journey

No creed or school of thought can monopolize the Spirit of God.

Oswald Chambers

Judging draws the judgment of others.

Catherine Marshall

Christians think they are prosecuting attorneys or judges, when, in reality, God has called all of us to be witnesses.

Warren Wiersbe

A Mother's Prayer

Dear Lord, sometimes I am quick to judge others. But, You have commanded me not to judge. Keep me mindful, Father, that when I judge others, I am living outside of Your will for my life. You have forgiven me, Lord. Let me forgive others, let me love them, and let me help them . . . without judging them. Amen

Being Grateful

Let the message about the Messiah dwell richly among you, teaching and admonishing one another in all wisdom, and singing psalms, hymns, and spiritual songs, with gratitude in your hearts to God.

Colossians 3:16 HCSB

For most of us, life is busy and complicated. We have countless responsibilities, some of which begin before sunrise and many of which end long after sunset. Amid the rush and crush of the daily grind, it is easy to lose sight of God and His blessings. But, when we forget to slow down and say "Thank You" to our Maker, we rob ourselves of His presence, His peace, and His joy.

Our task—as the leaders of our families and as believing Christians—is to praise God many times each day. Then, with gratitude in our hearts, we can face our daily duties with the perspective and power that only He can provide.

More from God's Word

Rejoice always, pray without ceasing, in everything give thanks; for this is the will of God in Christ Jesus for you.

1 Thessalonians 5:16-18 NKJV

Thanks be to God for His indescribable gift.

2 Corinthians 9:15 HCSB

Therefore as you have received Christ Jesus the Lord, walk in Him, rooted and built up in Him and established in the faith, just as you were taught, and overflowing with thankfulness.

Colossians 2:6-7 HCSB

Those who cling to worthless idols forsake faithful love, but as for me, I will sacrifice to You with a voice of thanksgiving. I will fulfill what I have vowed. Salvation is from the Lord!

Jonah 2:8-9 HCSB

Give thanks to the Lord, for He is good; His faithful love endures forever.

Psalm 118:29 HCSB

More Ideas for Your Journey

A sense of gratitude for God's presence in our lives will help open our eyes to what he has done in the past and what he will do in the future.

Emilie Barnes

Gratitude unlocks the fullness of life. It turns what we have into enough, and more. It turns denial into acceptance, chaos to order, confusion to clarity. It can turn a meal into a feast, a house into a home, a stranger into a friend. Gratitude makes sense of our past, brings peace for today, and creates a vision for tomorrow.

Melody Beattie

Gratitude changes the pangs of memory into a tranquil joy.

Dietrich Bonhoeffer

A Mother's Prayer

Lord, let my attitude be one of gratitude. You have given me much; when I think of Your grace and goodness, I am humbled and thankful. Today, let me express my thanksgiving, Father, not just through my words but also through my deeds . . . and may all the glory be Yours. Amen

Healthy Habits

Do you not know that your body is a sanctuary of the Holy Spirit who is in you, whom you have from God? You are not your own, for you were bought at a price; therefore glorify God in your body.

1 Corinthians 6:19-20 HCSB

It's an old saying and a true one: First, you make your habits, and then your habits make you. Some habits will inevitably bring you closer to God; other habits will lead you away from the path He has chosen for you. If you sincerely desire to improve your spiritual health, you must honestly examine the habits that make up the fabric of your day. And you must abandon those habits that are displeasing to God.

If you trust God, and if you keep asking for His help, He can transform your life. If you sincerely ask Him to help you, the same God who created the universe will help you defeat the harmful habits that have heretofore defeated you. So, if at first you don't succeed, keep praying. God is listening, and He's ready to help you become a better person if you ask Him . . . so ask today.

More from God's Word

Do not be deceived: "Evil company corrupts good habits."

1 Corinthians 15:33 NKJV

Guard your heart above all else, for it is the source of life.

Proverbs 4:23 HCSB

For we know that if our earthly house, a tent, is destroyed, we have a building from God, a house not made with hands, eternal in the heavens.

2 Corinthians 5:1 HCSB

For You formed my inward parts; You covered me in my mother's womb. I will praise You, for I am fearfully and wonderfully made; marvelous are Your works.

Psalm 139:13-14 NKJV

Don't copy the behavior and customs of this world, but let God transform you into a new person by changing the way you think. Then you will know what God wants you to do, and you will know how good and pleasing and perfect his will really is.

Romans 12:2 NLT

More Ideas for Your Journey

Since behaviors become habits, make them work with you and not against you.

E. Stanley Jones

Prayer is a habit. Worship is a habit. Kindness is a habit. And if you want to please God, you'd better make sure that these habits are your habits.

Marie T. Freeman

You will never change your life until you change something you do daily.

John Maxwell

A Mother's Prayer

Dear Lord, help me break bad habits and form good ones. And let my actions be pleasing to You, today and every day. Amen

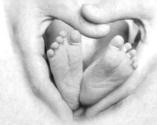

Imitating Christ

Therefore, be imitators of God, as dearly loved children.

Ephesians 5:1 HCSB

Imitating Christ is impossible, but attempting to imitate Him is both possible and advisable. By attempting to imitate Jesus, we seek, to the best of our abilities, to walk in His footsteps. To the extent we succeed in following Him, we receive the spiritual abundance that is the rightful possession of those who love Christ and keep His commandments.

Do you seek God's blessings for the day ahead? Then, to the best of your abilities, imitate His Son. You will fall short, of course. But if your heart is right and your intentions are pure, God will bless your efforts, your day, and your life.

More from God's Word

But whoever keeps His word, truly the love of God is perfected in him. By this we know that we are in Him. He who says he abides in Him ought himself also to walk just as He walked.

1 John 2:5-6 NKJV

Whoever serves me must follow me. Then my servant will be with me everywhere I am. My Father will honor anyone who serves me.

John 12:26 NCV

Then Jesus spoke to them again: "I am the light of the world. Anyone who follows Me will never walk in the darkness, but will have the light of life."

John 8:12 HCSB

Whoever is not willing to carry the cross and follow me is not worthy of me. Those who try to hold on to their lives will give up true life. Those who give up their lives for me will hold on to true life.

Matthew 10:38-39 NCV

More Ideas for Your Journey

The whole idea of belonging to Christ is to look less and less like we used to and more and more like Him.

Angela Thomas

You cannot cooperate with Jesus in becoming what He wants you to become and simultaneously be what the world desires to make you. If you would say, "Take the world but give me Jesus," then you must deny yourself and take up your cross. The simple truth is that your "self" must be put to death in order for you to get to the point where for you to live is Christ. What will it be? The world and you, or Jesus and you? You do have a choice to make.

Kay Arthur

Every Christian is to become a little Christ. The whole purpose of becoming a Christian is simply nothing else.

C. S. Lewis

A Mother's Prayer

Dear Lord, You sent Your Son so that I might have abundant life and eternal life. Thank You, Father, for my Savior, Christ Jesus. I will follow Him, honor Him, and share His Good News, this day and every day. Amen

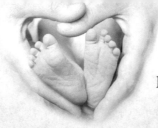

So Laugh!

There is a time for everything, and everything on earth has its special season. . . . There is a time to cry and a time to laugh. There is a time to be sad and a time to dance.

Ecclesiastes 3:1, 4 NCV

Laughter is a gift from God, a gift that He intends for us to use. Yet sometimes, because of the inevitable stresses of everyday living, we fail to find the fun in life. When we allow life's disappointments to cast a pall over our lives and our souls, we do a profound disservice to ourselves and to our loved ones.

If you've allowed the clouds of life to obscure the blessings of life, perhaps you've formed the unfortunate habit of taking things just a little too seriously. If so, it's time to fret a little less and laugh a little more.

So today, look for the humor that most certainly surrounds you—when you do, you'll find it. And remember: God created laughter for a reason . . . and Father indeed knows best. So laugh!

More Ideas for Your Journey

I want to encourage you in these days with your family to lighten up and enjoy. Laugh a little bit; it might just set you free.

Dennis Swanberg

As you're rushing through life, take time to stop a moment, look into people's eyes, say something kind, and try to make them laugh!

Barbara Johnson

He who laughs lasts—he who doesn't, doesn't.

Marie T. Freeman

A Mother's Prayer

Dear Lord, laughter is Your gift to me; help me to enjoy it. Today and every day, put a smile on my face, and help me to share that smile with other people, starting with my family. This is the day that You have made, Lord. Let me enjoy it . . . and let me laugh. Amen

Getting to Know Him

Be still, and know that I am God.

Psalm 46:10 NKJV

Do you ever wonder if God is really "right here, right now"? Do you wonder if God hears your prayers, if He understands your feelings, or if He really knows your heart? But when you have doubts, remember this: God isn't on a coffee break, and He hasn't moved out of town. He's right here, right now, listening to your thoughts and prayers, watching over your every move.

The Bible teaches that a wonderful way to get to know God is simply to be still and listen to Him. But sometimes, you may find it hard to slow down and listen. As the demands of everyday life weigh down upon you, you may be tempted to ignore God's presence or—worse yet—to rebel against His commandments. But, when you quiet yourself and acknowledge His presence, God touches your heart and restores your spirits. So why not let Him do it right now? If you really want to know Him better, silence is a wonderful place to start.

More from God's Word

You shall have no other gods before Me.

Exodus 20:3 NKJV

For it is written, "You shall worship the Lord your God, and Him only you shall serve."

Matthew 4:10 NKJV

The one who does not love does not know God, because God is love.

1 John 4:8 HCSB

God is Spirit, and those who worship Him must worship in spirit and truth.

John 4:24 HCSB

Draw near to God, and He will draw near to you.

James 4:8 HCSB

More Ideas for Your Journey

You cannot grow spiritually until you have the assurance that Christ is in your life.

Vonette Bright

Knowing God involves an intimate, personal relationship that is developed over time through prayer and getting answers to prayer, through Bible study and applying its teaching to our lives, through obedience and experiencing the power of God, through moment-by-moment submission to Him that results in a moment-by-moment filling of the Holy Spirit.

Anne Graham Lotz

Here is our opportunity: we cannot see God, but we can see Christ. Christ was not only the Son of God, but He was the Father. Whatever Christ was, that God is.

Hannah Whitall Smith

A Mother's Prayer

Dear Lord, help me remember the importance of silence. Help me discover quiet moments throughout the day so that I can sense Your presence and Your love. Amen

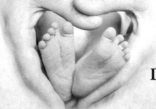

God's Timetable

Wait for the Lord; be courageous and let your heart be strong. Wait for the Lord.

Psalm 27:14 HCSB

If you sincerely seek to be a woman of faith, then you must learn to trust God's timing. You will be sorely tempted, however, to do otherwise. Because you are a fallible human being, you are impatient for things to happen. But, God knows better.

God has created a world that unfolds according to His own timetable, not ours . . . thank goodness! We mortals might make a terrible mess of things. God does not.

God's plan does not always happen in the way that we would like or at the time of our own choosing. Our task—as believing Christians who trust in a benevolent, all-knowing Father—is to wait patiently for God to reveal Himself. And reveal Himself He will. Always. But until God's perfect plan is made known, we must walk in faith and never lose hope. And we must continue to trust Him. Always.

More from God's Word

He said to them, "It is not for you to know times or periods that the Father has set by His own authority."

Acts 1:7 HCSB

He has made everything appropriate in its time. He has also put eternity in their hearts, but man cannot discover the work God has done from beginning to end.

Ecclesiastes 3:11 HCSB

Therefore the Lord is waiting to show you mercy, and is rising up to show you compassion, for the Lord is a just God. Happy are all who wait patiently for Him.

Isaiah 30:18 HCSB

For My thoughts are not your thoughts, and your ways are not My ways. For as heaven is higher than earth, so My ways are higher than your ways, and My thoughts than your thoughts.

Isaiah 55:8-9 HCSB

I waited patiently for the LORD; and He inclined to me, and heard my cry.

Psalm 40:1 NKJV

More Ideas for Your Journey

He has the right to interrupt your life. He is Lord. When you accepted Him as Lord, you gave Him the right to help Himself to your life anytime He wants.

Henry Blackaby

When there is perplexity there is always guidance—not always at the moment we ask, but in good time, which is God's time. There is no need to fret and stew.

Elisabeth Elliot

Your times are in His hands. He's in charge of the timetable, so wait patiently.

Kay Arthur

A Mother's Prayer

Lord, my sense of timing is fallible and imperfect; Yours is not. Let me trust in Your timetable for my life, and give me the patience and the wisdom to trust Your plans, not my own. Amen

Listening to God

The one who is from God listens to God's words. This is why you don't listen, because you are not from God.

John 8:47 HCSB

Sometimes God speaks loudly and clearly. More often, He speaks in a quiet voice—and if you are wise, you will be listening carefully when He does. To do so, you must carve out quiet moments each day to study His Word and sense His direction.

Can you quiet yourself long enough to listen to your conscience? Are you attuned to the subtle guidance of your intuition? Are you willing to pray sincerely and then to wait quietly for God's response? Hopefully so. Usually God refrains from sending His messages on stone tablets or city billboards. More often, He communicates in subtler ways. If you sincerely desire to hear His voice, you must listen carefully, and you must do so in the silent corners of your quiet, willing heart.

More from God's Word

Listen in silence before me....

Isaiah 41:1 NLT

God has no use for the prayers of the people who won't listen to him.

Proverbs 28:9 MSG

Trust God from the bottom of your heart; don't try to figure out everything on your own. Listen for God's voice in everything you do, everywhere you go; he's the one who will keep you on track.

Proverbs 3:5-6 MSG

You must follow the Lord your God and fear Him. You must keep His commands and listen to His voice; you must worship Him and remain faithful to Him.

Deuteronomy 13:4 HCSB

But as God has distributed to each one, as the Lord has called each one, so let him walk.

1 Corinthians 7:17 NKJV

More Ideas for Your Journey

God is always listening.

Stormie Omartian

When we come to Jesus stripped of pretensions, with a needy spirit, ready to listen, He meets us at the point of need.

Catherine Marshall

We cannot experience the fullness of Christ if we do all the expressing. We must allow God to express His love, will, and truth to us.

Gary Smalley

A Mother's Prayer

Father, in these quiet moments before this busy day unfolds, I come to You. May my meditations bring You pleasure just as surely as they bring me a clearer sense of Your love and Your peace. May the time I spend in quiet meditation mold my day and my life . . . for You. Amen

Love According to God

Now these three remain: faith, hope, and love. But the greatest of these is love.

1 Corinthians 13:13 HCSB

Love, like everything else in this wonderful world, begins and ends with God, but the middle part belongs to us. During the brief time that we have here on earth, God has given each of us the opportunity to become a loving person—or not. God has given each of us the opportunity to be kind, to be courteous, to be cooperative, and to be forgiving—or not. God has given each of us the chance to obey the Golden Rule, or to make up our own rules as we go. If we obey God's rules, we're safe, but if we do otherwise, we're headed for trouble and fast.

Here in the real world, the choices that we make have consequences. The decisions that we make and the results of those decisions determine the quality of our relationships. It's as simple as that.

More from God's Word

I pray that you, being rooted and firmly established in love, may be able to comprehend with all the saints what is the breadth and width, height and depth, and to know the Messiah's love that surpasses knowledge, so you may be filled with all the fullness of God.

Ephesians 3:17-19 HCSB

If I speak the languages of men and of angels, but do not have love, I am a sounding gong or a clanging cymbal.

1 Corinthians 13:1 HCSB

Dear friends, if God loved us in this way, we also must love one another.

1 John 4:11 HCSB

We love because He first loved us.

1 John 4:19 HCSB

Hatred stirs up conflicts, but love covers all offenses.

Proverbs 10:12 HCSB

More Ideas for Your Journey

Those who abandon ship the first time it enters a storm miss the calm beyond. And the rougher the storms weathered together, the deeper and stronger real love grows.

Ruth Bell Graham

It is when we come to the Lord in our nothingness, our powerlessness and our helplessness that He then enables us to love in a way which, without Him, would be absolutely impossible.

Elisabeth Elliot

Love is extravagant in the price it is willing to pay, the time it is willing to give, the hardships it is willing to endure, and the strength it is willing to spend. Love never thinks in terms of "how little," but always in terms of "how much." Love gives, love knows, and love lasts.

Joni Eareckson Tada

A Mother's Prayer

Dear Lord, today and every day, I will tell my family that I love them. And I will show my family that I love them. Amen

Patience NOW!

Be gentle to everyone, able to teach, and patient.

2 Timothy 2:23 HCSB

The rigors of motherhood can test the patience of the most even-tempered moms: From time to time, even the most mannerly children may do things that worry us, or confuse us, or anger us. Why? Because they are children, and because they are human.

As loving parents, we must be patient with our children's shortcomings (just as they, too, must be patient with our own). But our patience must not be restricted to those who live under our care. We must also strive, to the best of our abilities, to exercise patience in all our dealings, because our children are watching and learning.

Sometimes, patience is simply the price we pay for being responsible parents, and that's exactly as it should be. After all, think how patient our Heavenly Father has been with us.

More from God's Word

Rejoice in hope; be patient in affliction; be persistent in prayer.

Romans 12:12 HCSB

Now we exhort you, brethren, warn those who are unruly, comfort the fainthearted, uphold the weak, be patient with all.

1 Thessalonians 5:14 NKJV

Love is patient; love is kind.

1 Corinthians 13:4 HCSB

A patient spirit is better than a proud spirit.

Ecclesiastes 7:8 HCSB

Therefore the Lord is waiting to show you mercy, and is rising up to show you compassion, for the Lord is a just God. Happy are all who wait patiently for Him.

Isaiah 30:18 HCSB

More Ideas for Your Journey

Let me encourage you to continue to wait with faith. God may not perform a miracle, but He is trustworthy to touch you and make you whole where there used to be a hole.

Lisa Whelchel

If you want to hear God's voice clearly and you are uncertain, then remain in His presence until He changes that uncertainty. Often much can happen during this waiting for the Lord. Sometimes he changes pride into humility; doubt into faith and peace....

Corrie ten Boom

He makes us wait. He keeps us in the dark on purpose. He makes us walk when we want to run, sit still when we want to walk, for he has things to do in our souls that we are not interested in.

Elisabeth Elliot

A Mother's Prayer

Father, let me wait quietly for You. Let me live according to Your plan and according to Your timetable. When I am hurried, slow me down. Today, I want to be a patient Christian as I trust in You and in Your plan. Amen

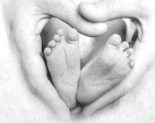

When You Have Doubts

Now if any of you lacks wisdom, he should ask God, who gives to all generously and without criticizing, and it will be given to him. But let him ask in faith without doubting. For the doubter is like the surging sea, driven and tossed by the wind.

James 1:5-6 HCSB

If you've never had any doubts about your faith, then you can stop reading this page now and skip to the next. But if you've ever been plagued by doubts about your faith or your God, keep reading.

Even some of the most faithful Christians are, at times, beset by occasional bouts of discouragement and doubt. But even when we feel far removed from God, God is never far removed from us. He is always with us, always willing to calm the storms of life—always willing to replace our doubts with comfort and assurance.

Whenever you're plagued by doubts, that's precisely the moment you should seek God's presence by genuinely seeking to establish a deeper, more meaningful relationship with His Son. Then you may rest assured that in time, God will calm your fears, answer your prayers, and restore your confidence.

More Ideas for Your Journey

Mark it down. God never turns away the honest seeker. Go to God with your questions. You may not find all the answers, but in finding God, you know the One who does.

Max Lucado

We are most vulnerable to the piercing winds of doubt when we distance ourselves from the mission and fellowship to which Christ has called us.

Joni Eareckson Tada

A Mother's Prayer

Dear Lord, when I am filled with uncertainty and doubt, give me faith. In the dark moments of life, keep me mindful of Your healing power and Your infinite love, so that I may live courageously and faithfully today and every day. Amen

Time for Fun

So I recommend having fun, because there is nothing better for people to do in this world than to eat, drink, and enjoy life. That way they will experience some happiness along with all the hard work God gives them.

Ecclesiastes 8:15 NLT

Are you a woman who takes time each day to really enjoy life? Hopefully so. After all, you are the recipient of a precious gift—the gift of life. And because God has seen fit to give you this gift, it is incumbent upon you to use it and to enjoy it. But sometimes, amid the inevitable pressures of everyday living, really enjoying life may seem almost impossible. It is not.

For most of us, fun is as much a function of attitude as it is a function of environment. So whether you're standing victorious atop one of life's mountains or trudging through one of life's valleys, enjoy yourself. You deserve to have fun today, and God wants you to have fun today . . . so what on earth are you waiting for?

More Ideas for Your Journey

Our thoughts, not our circumstances, determine our happiness.

John Maxwell

Whence comes this idea that if what we are doing is fun, it can't be God's will? The God who made giraffes, a baby's fingernails, a puppy's tail, a crooknecked squash, the bobwhite's call, and a young girl's giggle, has a sense of humor. Make no mistake about that.

Catherine Marshall

I became aware of one very important concept I had missed before: my attitude—not my circumstances—was what was making me unhappy.

Vonette Bright

A Mother's Prayer

Lord, make me a happy Christian. Let me rejoice in the gift of this day, and let me praise You for the gift of Your Son. Make me be a joyful teacher, Lord, as I share Your Good News with all those who need Your healing touch. Amen

No Shortcuts

In all the work you are doing, work the best you can. Work as if you were doing it for the Lord, not for people.

Colossians 3:23 NCV

Providing for a family requires work, and lots of it. And whether or not your work carries you outside the home, your good works have earned the gratitude of your loved ones and the praise of your Heavenly Father.

It has been said that there are no shortcuts to any place worth going. Making the grade in today's competitive workplace is not easy. In fact, it can be very difficult indeed. The same can be said for the important work that occurs within the four walls of your home.

God did not create you and your family for lives of mediocrity; He created you for far greater things. Accomplishing God's work is seldom easy. What's required is determination, persistence, patience, and discipline—which is perfectly fine with God. After all, He knows that you're up to the task, and He has big plans for all of you.

More from God's Word

Whatever your hands find to do, do with [all] your strength.

Ecclesiastes 9:10 HCSB

He did it with all his heart. So he prospered.

2 Chronicles 31:21 NKJV

Don't work only while being watched, in order to please men, but as slaves of Christ, do God's will from your heart. Render service with a good attitude, as to the Lord and not to men.

Ephesians 6:6-7 HCSB

We must do the works of Him who sent Me while it is day. Night is coming when no one can work.

John 9:4 HCSB

In fact, when we were with you, this is what we commanded you: "If anyone isn't willing to work, he should not eat."

2 Thessalonians 3:10 HCSB

More Ideas for Your Journey

Help yourself and God will help you.

St. Joan of Arc

How do I love God? By doing beautifully the work I have been given to do, by doing simply that which God entrusted to me, in whatever form it may take.

Mother Teresa

God does not want us to work for Him, nor does He want to be our helper. Rather, He wants to do His work in and through us.

Vonette Bright

A Mother's Prayer

Heavenly Father, You know that motherhood is difficult work. When I am tired, give me strength. When I become frustrated, give me patience. When I lose sight of Your purpose for my life, give me a passion for my daily responsibilities. Let me raise my children to be Your loving, faithful servants, and let all the honor and glory be Yours. Amen

Living Courageously

The Lord is the One who will go before you. He will be with you; He will not leave you or forsake you. Do not be afraid or discouraged.

Deuteronomy 31:8 HCSB

This world can be a dangerous and daunting place, but Christians have every reason to live courageously. After all, the ultimate battle has already been fought and won on the cross at Calvary. But even the most dedicated Christian mom may find her courage tested by the inevitable disappointments and fears that visit the lives of believers and non-believers alike.

The next time you find your courage tested to the limit, remember to take your fears to God. If you call upon Him, you will be comforted. Whatever your challenge, whatever your trouble, God can handle it. And will.

More from God's Word

Be strong and courageous, and do the work. Don't be afraid or discouraged, for the Lord God, my God, is with you. He won't leave you or forsake you.

1 Chronicles 28:20 HCSB

For God has not given us a spirit of fearfulness, but one of power, love, and sound judgment.

2 Timothy 1:7 HCSB

Be alert, stand firm in the faith, be brave and strong.

1 Corinthians 16:13 HCSB

Haven't I commanded you: be strong and courageous? Do not be afraid or discouraged, for the Lord your God is with you wherever you go.

Joshua 1:9 HCSB

But when Jesus heard it, He answered him, "Don't be afraid. Only believe."

Luke 8:50 HCSB

More Ideas for Your Journey

What is courage? It is the ability to be strong in trust, in conviction, in obedience. To be courageous is to step out in faith—to trust and obey, no matter what.

Kay Arthur

If a person fears God, he or she has no reason to fear anything else. On the other hand, if a person does not fear God, then fear becomes a way of life.

Beth Moore

When once we are assured that God is good, then there can be nothing left to fear.

Hannah Whitall Smith

A Mother's Prayer

Lord, at times, this world is a fearful place. I fear for my family and especially for my children. Yet, You have promised me that You are with me always. With You as my protector, I am not afraid. Today, Dear Lord, let me live courageously as I place my trust in You. Amen

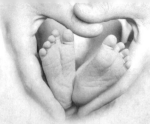

Running on Empty

But those who wait on the Lord shall renew their strength;
they shall mount up with wings like eagles, they shall run and
not be weary, they shall walk and not faint.

Isaiah 40:31 NKJV

God intends that His children lead joyous lives filled with abundance and peace. But sometimes, as all mothers can attest, abundance and peace seem very far away. It is then that we must turn to God for renewal, and when we do, He will restore us.

Have you "tapped in" to the power of God, or are you muddling along under your own power? If you are weary, worried, fretful or fearful, then it is time to turn to a strength much greater than your own.

The Bible tells us that we can do all things through the power of our risen Savior, Jesus Christ. Our challenge, then, is clear: we must place Christ where He belongs: at the very center of our lives.

Are you tired or troubled? Turn your heart toward God in prayer. Are you weak or worried? Make the time to delve deeply into God's Holy Word. When you do, you'll discover that the Creator of the universe stands ready and able to create a new sense of wonderment and joy in you.

More from God's Word

Therefore if anyone is in Christ, he is a new creature; the old things passed away; behold, new things have come.

2 Corinthians 5:17 HCSB

You are being renewed in the spirit of your minds; you put on the new man, the one created according to God's likeness in righteousness and purity of the truth.

Ephesians 4:23-24 HCSB

I will give you a new heart and put a new spirit within you.

Ezekiel 36:26 HCSB

Finally, brothers, rejoice. Be restored, be encouraged, be of the same mind, be at peace, and the God of love and peace will be with you.

2 Corinthians 13:11 HCSB

More Ideas for Your Journey

If you're willing to repair your life, God is willing to help. If you're not willing to repair your life, God is willing to wait.

Marie T. Freeman

He is the God of wholeness and restoration.

Stormie Omartian

But while relaxation is one thing, refreshment is another. We need to drink frequently and at length from God's fresh springs, to spend time in the Scripture, time in fellowship with Him, time worshiping Him.

Ruth Bell Graham

A Mother's Prayer

Lord, I am an imperfect mother. Sometimes, I become overwhelmed by the demands of the day. When I feel tired or discouraged, renew my strength. When I am worried, let me turn my thoughts and my prayers to You. Let me trust Your promises, Dear Lord, and let me accept Your unending love, now and forever. Amen

Being Generous

So let each one give as he purposes in his heart, not grudgingly or of necessity; for God loves a cheerful giver.

2 Corinthians 9:7 NKJV

God's gifts are beyond description, His blessings beyond comprehension. God has been incredibly generous with us, and He rightfully expects us to be generous with others. That's why the thread of generosity is woven into the very fabric of God's teachings.

In the Old Testament, we are told that, "The good person is generous and lends lavishly...." (Psalm 112:5 MSG). And in the New Testament we are instructed, "Freely you have received, freely give" (Matthew 10:8 NKJV). These principles still apply. As we establish priorities for our days and our lives, we are advised to give freely of our time, our possessions, and our love—just as God has given freely to us.

Of course, we can never fully repay God for His gifts, but we can share them with others. And we should.

More from God's Word

In every way I've shown you that by laboring like this, it is necessary to help the weak and to keep in mind the words of the Lord Jesus, for He said, "It is more blessed to give than to receive."

Acts 20:35 HCSB

Dear friend, you are showing your faith by whatever you do for the brothers, and this you are doing for strangers.

3 John 1:5 HCSB

Bear one another's burdens, and so fulfill the law of Christ.

Galatians 6:2 NKJV

If a brother or sister is without clothes and lacks daily food, and one of you says to them, "Go in peace, keep warm, and eat well," but you don't give them what the body needs, what good is it?

James 2:15–16 HCSB

The one who has two shirts must share with someone who has none, and the one who has food must do the same.

Luke 3:11 HCSB

More Ideas for Your Journey

Nothing is really ours until we share it.

C. S. Lewis

The measure of a life, after all, is not its duration but its donation.

Corrie ten Boom

We can't do everything, but can we do anything more valuable than invest ourselves in another?

Elisabeth Elliot

A Mother's Prayer

Lord, make me a generous and cheerful Christian. Let me be kind to those who need my encouragement, and let me share with those who need my help, today and every day. Amen

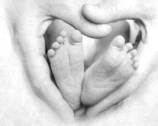

Following Jesus

Whoever serves me must follow me. Then my servant will be with me everywhere I am. My Father will honor anyone who serves me.

John 12:26 NCV

J esus walks with you. Are you walking with Him? Hopefully, you will choose to walk with Him today and every day of your life. And hopefully, you will encourage your family to do the same.

God's Word is clear: When we genuinely invite Christ to reign over our hearts, and when we accept His transforming love, we are forever changed. When we welcome Christ into our hearts, an old life ends and a new way of living—along with a completely new way of viewing the world—begins.

Each day offers a fresh opportunity to invite Christ, yet once again, to rule over our hearts and our days. Each morning presents yet another opportunity to take up His cross and follow in His footsteps. Today, let us rejoice in the new life that is ours through Christ, and let us follow Him, step by step, on the path that He first walked.

More from God's Word

But whoever keeps His word, truly in him the love of God is perfected. This is how we know we are in Him: the one who says he remains in Him should walk just as He walked.

1 John 2:5-6 HCSB

We encouraged, comforted, and implored each one of you to walk worthy of God, who calls you into His own kingdom and glory.

1 Thessalonians 2:12 HCSB

"Follow Me," Jesus told them, "and I will make you into fishers of men!" Immediately they left their nets and followed Him.

Mark 1:17-18 HCSB

You did not choose Me, but I chose you. I appointed you that you should go out and produce fruit, and that your fruit should remain, so that whatever you ask the Father in My name, He will give you.

John 15:16 HCSB

Then He said to them all, "If anyone wants to come with Me, he must deny himself, take up his cross daily, and follow Me."

Luke 9:23 HCSB

More Ideas for Your Journey

It's your heart that Jesus longs for: your will to be made His own with self on the cross forever, and Jesus alone on the throne.

Ruth Bell Graham

Jesus challenges you and me to keep our focus daily on the cross of His will if we want to be His disciples.

Anne Graham Lotz

The Christian faith is meant to be lived moment by moment. It isn't some broad, general outline—it's a long walk with a real Person. Details count: passing thoughts, small sacrifices, a few encouraging words, little acts of kindness, brief victories over nagging sins.

Joni Eareckson Tada

A Mother's Prayer

Dear Lord, You sent Jesus to save the world and to save me. I thank You for Jesus, and I will do my best to follow Him, today and forever. Amen

Trust the Shepherd

The Lord is my shepherd; I shall not want.

Psalm 23:1 KJV

In the 23rd Psalm, David teaches us that God is like a watchful shepherd caring for His flock. No wonder these verses have provided comfort and hope for generations of believers.

You are precious in the eyes of God. You are His priceless creation, made in His image, and protected by Him. God watches over every step you make and every breath you take, so you need never be afraid. But sometimes, fear has a way of slipping into the minds and hearts of even the most devout believers—and you are no exception.

As a busy woman, you know from firsthand experience that life is not always easy. But as a recipient of God's grace, you also know that you are protected by a loving Heavenly Father.

On occasion, you will confront circumstances that trouble you to the very core of your soul. When you are afraid, trust in God. When you are worried, turn your concerns over to Him. When you are anxious, be still and listen for the quiet assurance of God's promises. And then, place your life in His hands. He is your shepherd today and throughout eternity. Trust the Shepherd.

More Ideas for Your Journey

Christ reigns in his church as shepherd-king. He has supremacy, but it is the superiority of a wise and tender shepherd over his needy and loving flock. He commands and receives obedience, but it is willing obedience of well-cared-for-sheep, offered joyfully to their beloved Shepherd, whose voice they know so well. He rules by the force of love and the energy of goodness.

C. H. Spurgeon

Since the Lord is your shepherd, what are you worried about?

Marie T. Freeman

A Mother's Prayer

Lord, You are my Shepherd. You care for me; You comfort me; You watch over me; and You have saved me. I will praise You, Father, for Your glorious works, for Your protection, for Your love, and for Your Son. Amen

God's Guidance

The LORD says, "I will guide you along the best pathway for your life. I will advise you and watch over you."

Psalm 32:8 NLT

The Bible promises that God will guide you if you let Him. Your job, of course, is to let Him. But sometimes, you will be tempted to do otherwise. Sometimes, you'll be tempted to go along with the crowd; other times, you'll be tempted to do things your way, not God's way. When you feel those temptations, resist them.

What will you allow to guide you through the coming day: your own desires (or, for that matter, the desires of your friends)? Or will you allow God to lead the way? The answer should be obvious. You should let God be your guide. When you entrust your life to Him completely and without reservation, God will give you the strength to meet any challenge, the courage to face any trial, and the wisdom to live in His righteousness. So trust Him today and seek His guidance. When you do, your next step will be the right one.

More from God's Word

In all your ways acknowledge Him, and He shall direct your paths.

Proverbs 3:6 NKJV

Yet Lord, You are our Father; we are the clay, and You are our potter; we all are the work of Your hands.

Isaiah 64:8 HCSB

Lord, You are my lamp; the Lord illuminates my darkness.

2 Samuel 22:29 HCSB

Every morning he wakes me. He teaches me to listen like a student. The Lord God helps me learn . . . .

Isaiah 50:4-5 NCV

Teach me Your way, Lord, and I will live by Your truth. Give me an undivided mind to fear Your name.

Psalm 86:11 HCSB

More Ideas for Your Journey

We must always invite Jesus to be the navigator of our plans, desires, wills, and emotions, for He is the way, the truth, and the life.

Bill Bright

If we neglect the Bible, we cannot expect to benefit from the wisdom and direction that result from knowing God's Word.

Vonette Bright

It is a joy that God never abandons His children. He guides faithfully all who listen to His directions.

Corrie ten Boom

A Mother's Prayer

Dear Lord, today I will trust You more completely. I will lean upon Your understanding, not mine. And I will trust You to guide my steps along a path of Your choosing. Amen

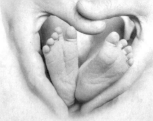

Too Busy?

Come to Me, all you who are weary and burdened, and I will give you rest. Take My yoke upon you and learn from Me, because I am gentle and humble in heart, and you will find rest for your souls. For My yoke is easy and My burden is light.

Matthew 11:28-30 HCSB

If you're a mom with too many responsibilities and too few hours in which to fulfill them, you are not alone. Motherhood is so demanding that sometimes you may feel as if you have no time for yourself . . . and no time for God.

Has the busy pace of life robbed you of the peace that might otherwise be yours through Jesus Christ? If so, you are simply too busy for your own good. Through His Son Jesus, God offers you a peace that passes human understanding, but He won't force His peace upon you; in order to experience it, you must slow down long enough to sense His presence and His love.

Today, as a gift to yourself, to your family, and to the world, slow down long enough to claim the inner peace that is your spiritual birthright: the peace of Jesus Christ. It is offered freely; it has been paid for in full; it is yours for the asking. So ask. And then share.

More from God's Word

Don't burn out; keep yourselves fueled and aflame. Be alert servants of the Master, cheerfully expectant. Don't quit in hard times; pray all the harder.

Romans 12:11-12 MSG

You can't go wrong when you love others. When you add up everything in the law code, the sum total is love. But make sure that you don't get so absorbed and exhausted in taking care of all your day-by-day obligations that you lose track of the time and doze off, oblivious to God.

Romans 13:10-11 MSG

Jesus said, "You're tied down to the mundane; I'm in touch with what is beyond your horizons. You live in terms of what you see and touch. I'm living on other terms. I told you that you were missing God in all this. You're at a dead end. If you won't believe I am who I say I am, you're at the dead end of sins. You're missing God in your lives."

John 8:23-24 MSG

More Ideas for Your Journey

In our tense, uptight society where folks are rushing to make appointments they have already missed, a good laugh can be as refreshing as a cup of cold water in the desert.

Barbara Johnson

The demand of every day kept me so busy that I subconsciously equated my busyness with commitment to Christ.

Vonette Bright

Frustration is not the will of God. There is time to do anything and everything that God wants us to do.

Elisabeth Elliot

A Mother's Prayer

Dear Lord, sometimes, I am distracted by the busyness of the day or the demands of the moment. When I am worried or anxious, Father, turn my thoughts back to You. Help me to trust Your will, to follow Your commands, and to accept Your peace, today and forever. Amen

Beyond Guilt

There is therefore now no condemnation to those who are in Christ Jesus, who do not walk according to the flesh, but according to the Spirit.

Romans 8:1 NKJV

All of us have made mistakes. Sometimes our failures result from our own shortsightedness. On other occasions, we are swept up in events that are beyond our abilities to control. Under either set of circumstances, we may experience intense feelings of guilt. But God has an answer for the guilt that we feel. That answer, of course, is His forgiveness.

When we ask our Heavenly Father for His forgiveness, He forgives us completely and without reservation. Then, we must do the difficult work of forgiving ourselves in the same way that God has forgiven us: thoroughly and unconditionally.

If you're feeling guilty, then it's time for a special kind of housecleaning—a housecleaning of your mind and your heart . . . beginning NOW!

More from God's Word

Be diligent to present yourself approved to God, a worker who doesn't need to be ashamed, correctly teaching the word of truth.

2 Timothy 2:15 HCSB

But God, who is abundant in mercy, because of His great love that He had for us, made us alive with the Messiah even though we were dead in trespasses. By grace you are saved!

Ephesians 2:4-5 HCSB

All the prophets testify about Him that through His name everyone who believes in Him will receive forgiveness of sins.

Acts 10:43 HCSB

Blessed be the God and Father of our Lord Jesus Christ, who according to His abundant mercy has begotten us again to a living hope through the resurrection of Jesus Christ from the dead....

1 Peter 1:3 NKJV

More Ideas for Your Journey

Identify the sin. Confess it. Turn from it. Avoid it at all costs. Live with a clean, forgiven conscience. Don't dwell on what God has forgotten!

Max Lucado

If God has forgiven you, why can't you forgive yourself?

Marie T. Freeman

Satan knows that if you live under a dark cloud of guilt, you will not be able to witness effectively or serve the Lord with power and blessing.

Warren Wiersbe

A Mother's Prayer

Dear Lord, thank You for the guilt that I feel when I disobey You. Help me confess my wrongdoings, help me accept Your forgiveness, and help me renew my passion to serve You. Amen

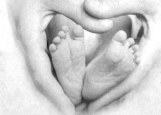

Finding Hope

Now may the God of hope fill you with all joy and peace in believing, so that you may overflow with hope by the power of the Holy Spirit.

Romans 15:13 HCSB

Are you a hope-filled mom? You should be. After all, God is good; His love endures; and He has offered you the priceless gift of eternal life. And, of course, God has blessed you with a loving family. But sometimes, in life's darker moments, you may lose sight of those blessings, and when you do, it's easy to lose hope.

When a suffering woman sought healing by merely touching the hem of His cloak, Jesus replied, "Daughter, be of good comfort; thy faith hath made thee whole" (Matthew 9:22 KJV). The message to believers is clear: if we are to be made whole by God, we must live by faith.

If you find yourself falling into the spiritual traps of worry and discouragement, seek the healing touch of Jesus and the encouraging words of fellow Christians. This world can be a place of trials and tribulations, but as believers, we are secure. Our hope is in God; He has promised us peace, joy, and eternal life. And, of course, God keeps His promises today, tomorrow, and forever, amen!

More from God's Word

But if we hope for what we do not see, we eagerly wait for it with patience.

Romans 8:25 HCSB

Rejoice in hope; be patient in affliction; be persistent in prayer.

Romans 12:12 HCSB

Lord, I turn my hope to You. My God, I trust in You. Do not let me be disgraced; do not let my enemies gloat over me.

Psalm 25:1-2 HCSB

Let us hold on to the confession of our hope without wavering, for He who promised is faithful.

Hebrews 10:23 HCSB

More Ideas for Your Journey

I discovered that sorrow was not to be feared but rather endured with hope and expectancy that God would use it to visit and bless my life.

Jill Briscoe

Hope must be in the future tense. Faith, to be faith, must always be in the present tense.

Catherine Marshall

Love is the seed of all hope. It is the enticement to trust, to risk, to try, and to go on.

Gloria Gaither

A Mother's Prayer

Today, Dear Lord, I will live in hope. If I become discouraged, I will turn to You. If I grow weary, I will seek strength in You. In every aspect of my life, I will trust You. You are my Father, Lord, and I place my hope and my faith in You. Amen

Believe in Miracles

Looking at them, Jesus said, "With men it is impossible, but not with God, because all things are possible with God."

Mark 10:27 HCSB

D o you believe that God is at work in the world? And do you also believe that nothing is impossible for Him? If so, then you also believe that God is perfectly capable of doing things that you, as a mere human being with limited vision and limited understanding, would deem to be utterly impossible. And that's precisely what God does.

Since the moment that He created our universe out of nothingness, God has made a habit of doing miraculous things. And He still works miracles today. Expect Him to work miracles in your own life, and then be watchful. With God, absolutely nothing is impossible, including an amazing assortment of miracles that He stands ready, willing, and able to perform for you and yours.

More from God's Word

I assure you: The one who believes in Me will also do the works that I do. And he will do even greater works than these, because I am going to the Father.

John 14:12 HCSB

But as it is written: "Eye has not seen, nor ear heard, nor have entered into the heart of man the things which God has prepared for those who love Him."

1 Corinthians 2:9 NKJV

For nothing will be impossible with God.

Luke 1:37 HCSB

You are the God who works wonders; You revealed Your strength among the peoples.

Psalm 77:14 HCSB

Is anything impossible for the Lord?

Genesis 18:14 HCSB

More Ideas for Your Journey

God specializes in things thought impossible.

Catherine Marshall

I could go through this day oblivious to the miracles all around me or I could tune in and "enjoy."

Gloria Gaither

Faith means believing in realities that go beyond sense and sight. It is the awareness of unseen divine realities all around you.

Joni Eareckson Tada

A Mother's Prayer

Lord, for You, nothing is impossible. Let me trust in Your power to do the miraculous, and let me trust in Your willingness to work miracles in my life—and in my heart. Amen

Energy for Today

Those who hope in the LORD will renew their strength. They will soar on wings like eagles; they will run and not grow weary, they will walk and not be faint.

Isaiah 40:31 NIV

If you're a mother with too many demands and too few hours in which to meet them, you are not alone. Motherhood is perhaps the world's most demanding profession. But don't fret: even when it seems that your responsibilities are simply too great to bear, you and God, working together, can handle them. So focus, not upon the difficulties of your circumstances, but instead upon God and upon His love for you. Then, ask Him for the strength that you need to fulfill your daily duties.

When you turn your thoughts and prayers to your Heavenly Father, He will give you the energy and the perspective to complete the most important items on your to-do list. And then, once you've done your best, leave the rest up to God. He can handle it . . . and will.

More from God's Word

Whatever you do, do it enthusiastically, as something done for the Lord and not for men.

Colossians 3:23 HCSB

Never be lazy in your work, but serve the Lord enthusiastically.

Romans 12:11 NLT

Whatever work you do, do your best, because you are going to the grave, where there is no working . . . .

Ecclesiastes 9:10 NCV

I have seen that there is nothing better than for a person to enjoy his activities, because that is his reward. For who can enable him to see what will happen after he dies?

Ecclesiastes 3:22 HCSB

Do your work with enthusiasm. Work as if you were serving the Lord, not as if you were serving only men and women.

Ephesians 6:7 NCV

More Ideas for Your Journey

I wish I could make it all new again; I can't. But God can. "He restores my soul," wrote the shepherd. God doesn't reform; he restores. He doesn't camouflage the old; he restores the new. The Master Builder will pull out the original plan and restore it. He will restore the vigor, he will restore the energy. He will restore the hope. He will restore the soul.

Max Lucado

Worry does not empty tomorrow of its sorrow; it empties today of its strength.

Corrie ten Boom

A Mother's Prayer

Lord, let me find my strength in You. When I am weary, give me rest. When I feel overwhelmed, let me look to You for my priorities. Let Your power be my power, Lord, and let Your way be my way, today and forever. Amen

Beyond Fear

Even when I go through the darkest valley, I fear [no] danger, for You are with me.

Psalm 23:4 HCSB

We live in a world that is, at times, a frightening place. We live in a world that is, at times, a discouraging place. We live in a world where life-changing losses can be so painful and so profound that it seems we will never recover. But, with God's help, and with the help of encouraging family members and friends, we can recover.

During the darker days of life, we are wise to remember the words of Jesus, who reassured His disciples, saying, "Take courage! It is I. Don't be afraid" (Matthew 14:27 NIV). Then, with God's comfort and His love in our hearts, we can offer encouragement to others. And by helping them face their fears, we can, in turn, tackle our own problems with courage, determination, and faith.

More from God's Word

Don't be afraid. Only believe.

Mark 5:36 HCSB

For I, the Lord your God, hold your right hand and say to you: Do not fear, I will help you.

Isaiah 41:13 HCSB

I sought the Lord, and He heard me, and delivered me from all my fears.

Psalm 34:4 NKJV

Do not fear, for I am with you; do not be afraid, for I am your God. I will strengthen you; I will help you; I will hold on to you with My righteous right hand.

Isaiah 41:10 HCSB

Indeed, God is my salvation. I will trust [Him] and not be afraid.

Isaiah 12:2 HCSB

More Ideas for Your Journey

Worry is a cycle of inefficient thoughts whirling around a center of fear.

Corrie ten Boom

Fear and doubt are conquered by a faith that rejoices. And faith can rejoice because the promises of God are as certain as God Himself.

Kay Arthur

When once we are assured that God is good, then there can be nothing left to fear.

Hannah Whitall Smith

A Mother's Prayer

Dear Lord, when I am fearful, keep me mindful that You are my protector and my salvation. Thank You, Father, for a perfect love that casts out fear. Because of You, I can live courageously and faithfully this day and every day. Amen

Using God's Gifts

Do not neglect the gift that is in you.

1 Timothy 4:14 HCSB

Your talents are a gift from God. And, the same applies to your children. Their talents, too, are blessings from the Creator, blessings which must be nurtured or forfeited.

Are you and your loved ones willing to use your gifts in the way that God intends? Are you willing to summon the discipline that is required to develop your talents and to hone your skills? That's precisely what God wants you to do, and that's precisely what you should desire for yourselves.

So be faithful stewards of your talents and treasures. And then prepare yourselves for even greater blessings that are sure to come.

More from God's Word

Each one has his own gift from God, one in this manner and another in that.

1 Corinthians 7:7 NKJV

Every generous act and every perfect gift is from above, coming down from the Father of lights.

James 1:17 HCSB

I remind you to keep ablaze the gift of God that is in you.

2 Timothy 1:6 HCSB

According to the grace given to us, we have different gifts: If prophecy, use it according to the standard of faith; if service, in service; if teaching, in teaching; if exhorting, in exhortation; giving, with generosity; leading, with diligence; showing mercy, with cheerfulness.

Romans 12:6-8 HCSB

Based on the gift they have received, everyone should use it to serve others, as good managers of the varied grace of God.

1 Peter 4:10 HCSB

More Ideas for Your Journey

Not everyone possesses boundless energy or a conspicuous talent. We are not equally blessed with great intellect or physical beauty or emotional strength. But we have all been given the same ability to be faithful.

Gigi Graham Tchividjian

The Lord has abundantly blessed me all of my life. I'm not trying to pay Him back for all of His wonderful gifts; I just realize that He gave them to me to give away.

Lisa Whelchel

God has given you special talents—now it's your turn to give them back to God.

Marie T. Freeman

A Mother's Prayer

Lord, I praise You for Your priceless gifts. I give thanks for Your creation, for Your Son, and for the unique talents and opportunities that You have given me. Let me use my gifts for the glory of Your kingdom, this day and every day. Amen

Share Your Optimism

My cup runs over. Surely goodness and mercy shall follow me all the days of my life; and I will dwell in the house of the Lord Forever.

Psalm 23:5-6 NKJV

Because you are a conscientious mom living in a difficult world, you may find yourself pulled down by the inevitable demands and worries of everyday life in the 21st century. Ours is a world brimming with temptations, distractions, and dangers. Sometimes, we can't help ourselves: we worry for our families, and we worry for ourselves.

If you become discouraged, exhausted, or both, then it's time to take your concerns to God. Whether you find yourself at the pinnacle of the mountain or the darkest depths of the valley, God is there. Open your heart to Him and He will lift your spirits and renew your strength.

Today, as a gift to your family and yourself, why not claim the joy that is rightfully yours in Christ? Why not take time to celebrate God's glorious creation? Why not trust your hopes instead of your fears? When you do, you

will think optimistically about yourself and your world
. . . and you can then share your optimism with others.
They'll be better for it, and so will you. But not necessarily in that order.

More from God's Word

Make me hear joy and gladness.

Psalm 51:8 NKJV

*But if we hope for what we do not see, we eagerly wait for it
with patience.*

Romans 8:25 HCSB

*For God has not given us a spirit of fearfulness, but one of
power, love, and sound judgment.*

2 Timothy 1:7 HCSB

I am able to do all things through Him who strengthens me.

Philippians 4:13 HCSB

More Ideas for Your Journey

Make the least of all that goes and the most of all that comes. Don't regret what is past. Cherish what you have. Look forward to all that is to come. And most important of all, rely moment by moment on Jesus Christ.

Gigi Graham Tchividjian

The Christian lifestyle is not one of legalistic do's and don'ts, but one that is positive, attractive, and joyful.

Vonette Bright

If you can't tell whether your glass is half-empty or half-full, you don't need another glass; what you need is better eyesight . . . and a more thankful heart.

Marie T. Freeman

A Mother's Prayer

Dear Lord, I will look for the best in other people, I will expect the best from You, and I will try my best to do my best—today and every day. Amen

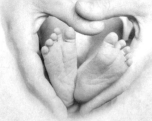

At Peace with the Past

Do not remember the past events, pay no attention to things of old. Look, I am about to do something new; even now it is coming. Do you not see it? Indeed, I will make a way in the wilderness, rivers in the desert.

Isaiah 43:18-19 HCSB

Have you made peace with your past? If so, congratulations. But, if you are mired in the quicksand of regret, it's time to plan your escape. How can you do so? By accepting what has been and by trusting God for what will be.

Because you are human, you may be slow to forget yesterday's disappointments; if so you are not alone. But if you sincerely seek to focus your hopes and energies on the future, then you must find ways to accept the past, no matter how difficult it may be to do so.

If you have not yet made peace with the past, today is the day to declare an end to all hostilities. When you do, you can then turn your thoughts to wondrous promises of God and to the glorious future that He has in store for you.

More Ideas for Your Journey

Shake the dust from your past, and move forward in His promises.

Kay Arthur

Whoever you are, whatever your condition or circumstance, whatever your past or problem, Jesus can restore you to wholeness.

Anne Graham Lotz

Yesterday is just experience but tomorrow is glistening with purpose—and today is the channel leading from one to the other.

Barbara Johnson

A Mother's Prayer

Heavenly Father, free me from anger, resentment, and envy. When I am bitter, I cannot feel the peace that You intend for my life. Keep me mindful that forgiveness is Your commandment, and help me accept the past, treasure the present, and trust the future . . . to You. Amen

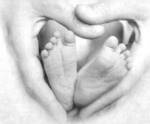

Your Bright Future

> *"I say this because I know what I am planning for you," says the Lord. "I have good plans for you, not plans to hurt you. I will give you hope and a good future."*
>
> *Jeremiah 29:11 NCV*

Because we are saved by a risen Christ, we can have hope for the future, no matter how troublesome our present circumstances may seem. Of course, we will face disappointments and failures while we are here on earth, but these are only temporary defeats. Of course, this world can be a place of trials and tribulations, but when we place our trust in the Giver of all things good, we are secure. God has promised us peace, joy, and eternal life. And God keeps His promises today, tomorrow, and forever.

Are you willing to place your future in the hands of a loving and all-knowing God? Do you trust in the ultimate goodness of His plan for your life? Will you face today's challenges with optimism and hope? You should. After all, God created you for a very important purpose:

His purpose. And you still have important work to do: His work.

Today, as you live in the present and look to the future, remember that God has a plan for you. Act—and believe—accordingly.

More from God's Word

Do not boast about tomorrow, for you do not know what a day may bring forth.

Proverbs 27:1 NKJV

For now we see indistinctly, as in a mirror, but then face to face. Now I know in part, but then I will know fully, as I am fully known.

1 Corinthians 13:12 HCSB

However, each one must live his life in the situation the Lord assigned when God called him.

1 Corinthians 7:17 HCSB

The earth and everything in it, the world and its inhabitants, belong to the Lord.

Psalm 24:1 HCSB

More Ideas for Your Journey

Joy comes from knowing God loves me and knows who I am and where I'm going . . . that my future is secure as I rest in Him.

James Dobson

The future lies all before us. Shall it only be a slight advance upon what we usually do? Ought it not to be a bound, a leap forward to altitudes of endeavor and success undreamed of before?

Annie Armstrong

Do not limit the limitless God! With Him, face the future unafraid because you are never alone.

Mrs. Charles E. Cowman

A Mother's Prayer

Dear Lord, as I look to the future, I will place my trust in You. If I become discouraged, I will turn to You. If I am afraid, I will seek strength in You. You are my Father, and I will place my hope, my trust, and my faith in You. Amen

Sharing His Peace

And the peace of God, which surpasses every thought, will guard your hearts and your minds in Christ Jesus. Finally brothers, whatever is true, whatever is honorable, whatever is just, whatever is pure, whatever is lovely, whatever is commendable—if there is any moral excellence and if there is any praise—dwell on these things.

Philippians 4:7-8 HCSB

The beautiful words of John 14:27 give us hope: "Peace I leave with you, my peace I give unto you . . . ." Jesus offers us peace, not as the world gives, but as He alone gives. We, as believers, can accept His peace or ignore it.

When we accept the peace of Jesus Christ into our hearts, our lives are transformed. And then, because we possess the gift of peace, we can share that gift with fellow Christians, family members, friends, and associates. If, on the other hand, we choose to ignore the gift of peace—for whatever reason—we cannot share what we do not possess.

As every woman knows, peace can be a scarce commodity in our demanding world. How, then, can we find the peace that we so desperately desire? By turning our days and our lives over to God. Elisabeth Elliot writes, "If my life is surrendered to God, all is well. Let me not grab it back, as though it were in peril in His hand but would be safer in mine!" May we give our lives, our hopes, and our prayers to the Lord, and, by doing so, accept His will and His peace.

More from God's Word

Abundant peace belongs to those who love Your instruction; nothing makes them stumble.

Psalm 119:165 HCSB

Blessed are the peacemakers, for they shall be called sons of God.

Matthew 5:9 NKJV

And suddenly there was with the angel a multitude of the heavenly host praising God and saying: "Glory to God in the highest, and on earth peace, goodwill toward men!"

Luke 2:13-14 NKJV

More Ideas for Your Journey

The fruit of our placing all things in God's hands is the presence of His abiding peace in our hearts.

Hannah Whitall Smith

God's peace is like a river, not a pond. In other words, a sense of health and well-being, both of which are expressions of the Hebrew *shalom,* can permeate our homes even when we're in white-water rapids.

Beth Moore

Let's please God by actively seeking, through prayer, "peaceful and quiet lives" for ourselves, our spouses, our children and grandchildren, our friends, and our nation (1 Timothy 2:1-3 NIV).

Shirley Dobson

A Mother's Prayer

Dear Lord, I will open my heart to You. And I thank You, God, for Your love, for Your peace, and for Your Son. Amen

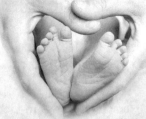

A Treasure from God

Train up a child in the way he should go, and when he is old he will not depart from it.

Proverbs 22:6 NKJV

As a mother, you are keenly aware that God has entrusted you with a priceless treasure from above: your child. Every child is different, yet every child is similar in this respect: every child is a glorious gift from above—and with that gift comes immense responsibilities.

Thoughtful mothers (like you) understand the critical importance of raising their children with love, with family, with discipline, and with God. By making God a focus in the home, loving mothers offer a priceless legacy to their children—a legacy of hope, a legacy of love, a legacy of wisdom.

Today, let us pray for our children . . . all of them. Let us pray for our own children and for children around the world. Every child is God's child. May we, as concerned mothers, behave—and pray—accordingly.

More from God's Word

When Jesus realized how much this mattered to them, he brought a child to his side. "Whoever accepts this child as if the child were me, accepts me," he said. "And whoever accepts me, accepts the One who sent me. You become great by accepting, not asserting. Your spirit, not your size, makes the difference."

Luke 9:47-48 MSG

Love the Lord your God with all your heart, with all your soul, and with all your strength. These words that I am giving you today are to be in your heart. Repeat them to your children. Talk about them when you sit in your house and when you walk along the road, when you lie down and when you get up.

Deuteronomy 6:5-7 HCSB

I have no greater joy than this: to hear that my children are walking in the truth.

3 John 1:4 HCSB

I assure you: Whoever does not welcome the kingdom of God like a little child will never enter it.

Luke 18:17 HCSB

More Ideas for Your Journey

He intended families to be the safe haven where children are born and raised, a place where the tender shoots are nurtured until their roots grow strong and deep.

Carol Kuykendall

Our faithfulness, or lack of it, will have an overwhelming impact on the heritage of our children.

Beth Moore

Any child will learn to worship God who lives his daily life with adults who worship Him.

Anna B. Mow

A Mother's Prayer

Lord, You have given me a wonderful responsibility: caring for my children. Let me love them, care for them, nurture them, teach them, and lead them to You. When I am weary, give me strength. When I am frustrated, give me patience. And, let my words and deeds always demonstrate to my children the love that I feel for them... and for You. Amen

Considering the Cross

But as for me, I will never boast about anything except the cross of our Lord Jesus Christ, through whom the world has been crucified to me, and I to the world.

Galatians 6:14 HCSB

As we consider Christ's sacrifice on the cross, we should be profoundly humbled and profoundly grateful. And today, as we come to Christ in prayer, we should do so in a spirit of quiet, heartfelt devotion to the One who gave His life so that we might have life eternal.

He was the Son of God, but He wore a crown of thorns. He was the Savior of mankind, yet He was put to death on the cross. He offered His healing touch to an unsaved world, and yet the same hands that had healed the sick and raised the dead were pierced with nails.

Christ humbled Himself on a cross—for you. He shed His blood—for you. He has offered to walk with you through this life and throughout all eternity. As you approach Him today in prayer, think about His sacrifice and His grace. And be humble.

More Ideas for Your Journey

Jesus challenges you and me to keep our focus daily on the cross of His will if we want to be His disciples.

Anne Graham Lotz

God is my heavenly Father. He loves me with an everlasting love. The proof of that is the Cross.

Elisabeth Elliot

The cross takes care of the past. The cross takes care of the flesh. The cross takes care of the world.

Kay Arthur

A Mother's Prayer

Dear Jesus, You are my Savior and my protector. You suffered on the cross for me, and I will give You honor and praise every day of my life. I will honor You with my words, my thoughts, and my prayers. And I will live according to Your commandments, so that through me, others might come to know Your perfect love. Amen

Beyond Failure

Even though good people may be bothered by trouble seven times, they are never defeated.

Proverbs 24:16 NCV

The occasional disappointments and failures of life are inevitable. Such setbacks are simply the price that we must occasionally pay for our willingness to take risks as we follow our dreams. But even when we encounter bitter disappointments, we must never lose faith.

As parents, we are far from perfect. And, without question, our children are imperfect as well. When we make mistakes, we must correct them and learn from them. And, when our children make mistakes, we must help them do likewise.

More Ideas for Your Journey

To have failed is to own more wisdom, understanding, and experience than do those who sit on life's sidelines playing it safe.

Susan Lenzkes

The difference between winning and losing is how we choose to react to disappointment.

Barbara Johnson

One of the ways God refills us after failure is through the blessing of Christian fellowship. Just experiencing the joy of simple activities shared with other children of God can have a healing effect on us.

Anne Graham Lotz

A Mother's Prayer

Dear Lord, when I encounter failures and disappointments, keep me mindful that You are in control. Let me persevere—even if my soul is troubled—and let me follow Your Son, Jesus Christ, this day and forever. Amen

Discipline Has Rewards

God hasn't invited us into a disorderly, unkempt life but into something holy and beautiful—as beautiful on the inside as the outside.

1 Thessalonians 4:7 MSG

Wise mothers teach their children the importance of discipline using their words and their examples. Disciplined moms understand that God doesn't reward laziness or misbehavior. To the contrary, God expects His believers to lead lives that are above reproach.

It has been said that there are no shortcuts to any place worth going. Thoughtful mothers agree. In Proverbs 28:19, God's message is clear: "He who works his land will have abundant food, but the one who chases fantasies will have his fill of poverty" (NIV).

When we work diligently and consistently, we can expect a bountiful harvest. But we must never expect the harvest to precede the labor. First, we must lead lives of discipline and obedience; then, we will reap the never-ending rewards that God has promised.

More Ideas for Your Journey

If I could just hang in there, being faithful to my own tasks, God would make me joyful and content. The responsibility is mine, but the power is His.

Peg Rankin

Real freedom means to welcome the responsibility it brings, to welcome the God-control it requires, to welcome the discipline that results, to welcome the maturity it creates.

Eugenia Price

God "longs to be gracious" to us (Isaiah 30:18), and He carries out His judgment against our sin with holy sorrow, intending His discipline to be a vehicle of mercy toward us.

Nancy Groom

A Mother's Prayer

Lord, let me be a disciplined parent, and let me teach my children to lead disciplined lives. Let me be Your faithful servant, Lord, and let me teach faithfulness by my conduct and by my communications. Let me raise my family in the knowledge of Your Word, and let me follow Your commandments just as surely as I teach my children to obey You and to love You. Amen

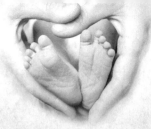

Happiness Now

But happy are those . . . whose hope is in the LORD their God.

Psalm 146:5 NLT

Okay, Mom, it's been a typical day. You've cared for your family, worked your fingers to the bone, rushed from point A to point Z, and taken barely a moment for yourself. But have you taken time to smile? If so, you're a very wise woman. If not, it's time to slow down, to take a deep breath, and to recount your blessings!

God has promised all of us the opportunity to experience spiritual abundance and peace. But it's up to each of us to claim the spiritual riches that God has in store. God promises us a life of fulfillment and joy, but He does not force His joy upon us.

Would you like to experience the peace and the joy that God intends for you? Then accept His Son and lay claim to His promises. Then, when you put a smile on your face that stretches all the way down to your heart, you'll discover that God smiles back.

More Ideas for Your Journey

Christ is the secret, the source, the substance, the center, and the circumference of all true and lasting gladness.

Mrs. Charles E. Cowman

I became aware of one very important concept I had missed before: my attitude—not my circumstances—was what was making me unhappy.

Vonette Bright

I am truly happy with Jesus Christ. I couldn't live without Him.

Ruth Bell Graham

A Mother's Prayer

Lord, let me be a mother who celebrates life. Let me rejoice in the gift of this day, and let me praise You for the gift of Your Son. Let me be a joyful Christian, Lord, as I share Your Good News with friends, with family, and with the world. Amen

Age and Beauty

Teach us to number our days carefully so that we may develop wisdom in our hearts.

Psalm 90:12 HCSB

We live in a society that glorifies youth. The messages that we receive from the media are unrelenting: We are told that we must do everything within our power to retain youthful values and a youthful appearance. The goal, we are told, is to remain "forever young"—yet this goal is not only unrealistic, but it is also unworthy of women who understand what genuine beauty is, and what it isn't. When it comes to "health and beauty" . . . you should focus more on health than on beauty. In fact, when you take care of your physical, spiritual, and mental health, your appearance will tend to take care of itself. And remember: God loves you during every stage of life—so embrace the aging process for what it is: an opportunity to grow closer to your loved ones and to your Creator.

More Ideas for Your Journey

Youth and age touch only the surface of our lives.

C. S. Lewis

Don't talk of growing old. If you continually talk of it, you may bring it on.

Hannah Whitall Smith

Youth is not a time of life but a state of mind. It boldly takes risks, seeks adventure, hopes for the best, and displays courage. You are as young as your faith is strong.

Barbara Johnson

A Mother's Prayer

Dear Lord, through every stage of life, I will praise You for Your blessings, for Your love, and for Your Son. Let me be a joyful believer every day of my life. Amen

A Mother's Mission

Commit your activities to the Lord and your plans will be achieved.

Proverbs 16:3 HCSB

Whether you realize it or not, you are on a personal mission for God. As a Christian mother, that mission is straightforward: Honor God, accept Christ as your Savior, raise your children in a loving, Christ-centered home, and be a servant to those who cross your path.

Of course, you will encounter impediments as you attempt to discover the exact nature of God's purpose for your life, but you must never lose sight of the overriding purposes that God has established for all believers. You will encounter these overriding purposes again and again as you worship your Creator and study His Word.

Every day offers countless opportunities to serve God and to worship Him. When you do so, He will bless you in miraculous ways. May you continue to seek God's will, may you trust His Word, and may you place Him where He belongs: at the very center of your life.

More from God's Word

For it is God who is working among you both the willing and the working for His good purpose.

Philippians 2:13 HCSB

We know that all things work together for the good of those who love God: those who are called according to His purpose.

Romans 8:28 HCSB

I will instruct you and show you the way to go; with My eye on you, I will give counsel.

Psalm 32:8 HCSB

You reveal the path of life to me; in Your presence is abundant joy; in Your right hand are eternal pleasures.

Psalm 16:11 HCSB

You are the light of the world.

Matthew 5:14 NIV

More Ideas for Your Journey

I am more and more persuaded that all that is required of us is faithful seed-sowing. The harvest is bound to follow.

Annie Armstrong

Forgetting your mission leads, inevitably, to getting tangled up in details—details that can take you completely off your path.

Laurie Beth Jones

You cannot walk through life without a dream or a destination and expect to arrive just where you wanted to go.

Lisa Bevere

A Mother's Prayer

Dear Lord, let Your purposes be my purposes. Let Your priorities be my priorities. Let Your will be my will. Let Your Word be my guide. And, let me grow in faith and in wisdom today and every day. Amen

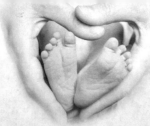

Give Encouragement

But encourage each other daily, while it is still called today, so that none of you is hardened by sin's deception.

Hebrews 3:13 HCSB

Your loved ones need a regular supply of encouraging words and pats on the back. And you need the rewards that God gives to enthusiastic moms who are a continual source of encouragement to their families.

The 118th Psalm reminds us, "This is the day which the Lord hath made; we will rejoice and be glad in it" (v. 24 KJV). As we rejoice in this day that the Lord has given us, let us remember that an important part of today's celebration is the time we spend celebrating others. Each day provides countless opportunities to encourage others and to praise their good works. When we do, we not only spread seeds of joy and happiness, we also follow the commandments of God's Holy Word.

Today, look for the good in others—starting with your loved ones. And then, celebrate the good that you find. When you do, you'll be a powerful force of encouragement in your corner of the world . . . and a worthy servant to your God.

More from God's Word

Therefore encourage one another and build each other up as you are already doing.

1 Thessalonians 5:11 HCSB

I want their hearts to be encouraged and joined together in love, so that they may have all the riches of assured understanding, and have the knowledge of God's mystery—Christ.

Colossians 2:2 HCSB

Carry one another's burdens; in this way you will fulfill the law of Christ.

Galatians 6:2 HCSB

And let us be concerned about one another in order to promote love and good works.

Hebrews 10:24 HCSB

More Ideas for Your Journey

Encouraging others means helping people, looking for the best in them, and trying to bring out their positive qualities.

John Maxwell

Words. Do you fully understand their power? Can any of us really grasp the mighty force behind the things we say? Do we stop and think before we speak, considering the potency of the words we utter?

Joni Eareckson Tada

As you're rushing through life, take time to stop a moment, look into people's eyes, say something kind, and try to make them laugh!

Barbara Johnson

A Mother's Prayer

Dear Lord, help me be a thoughtful mother and a genuine source of encouragement to my family. Just as You have lifted me up, let me also lift up my loved ones with a spirit of enthusiasm and hope. Amen

God's Promises

*Let us hold on to the confession of our hope without wavering,
for He who promised is faithful.*

Hebrews 10:23 HCSB

The Bible contains promises, made by God, upon which we, as believers, can and must depend. But sometimes, especially when we find ourselves caught in the inevitable entanglements of life, we fail to trust God completely.

Are you tired? Discouraged? Fearful? Be comforted and trust the promises that God has made to you. Are you worried or anxious? Be confident in God's power. Do you see a difficult future ahead? Be courageous and call upon God. He will protect you and then use you according to His purposes. Are you confused? Listen to the quiet voice of your Heavenly Father. He is not a God of confusion. Talk with Him; listen to Him; trust Him, and trust His promises. He is steadfast, and He is your Protector . . . forever.

More Ideas for Your Journey

Shake the dust from your past, and move forward in His promises.

Kay Arthur

We have ample evidence that the Lord is able to guide. The promises cover every imaginable situation. All we need to do is to take the hand he stretches out.

Elisabeth Elliot

Claim all of God's promises in the Bible. Your sins, your worries, your life—you may cast them all on Him.

Corrie ten Boom

A Mother's Prayer

Lord, Your Holy Word contains promises, and I will trust them. I will use the Bible as my guide, and I will trust You, Lord, to speak to me through Your Holy Spirit and through Your Holy Word, this day and forever. Amen

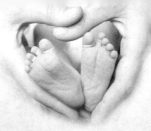

Real Repentance

Come back to the LORD and live!

Amos 5:6 NLT

Who among us has sinned? All of us. But, God calls upon us to turn away from sin by following His commandments. And the good news is this: When we do ask God's forgiveness and turn our hearts to Him, He forgives us absolutely and completely.

Genuine repentance requires more than simply offering God apologies for our misdeeds. Real repentance may start with feelings of sorrow and remorse, but it ends only when we turn away from the sin that has heretofore distanced us from our Creator. In truth, we offer our most meaningful apologies to God, not with our words, but with our actions. As long as we are still engaged in sin, we may be "repenting," but we have not fully "repented."

Is there an aspect of your life that is distancing you from your God? If so, ask for His forgiveness, and—just as importantly—stop sinning. Then, wrap yourself in the protection of God's Word. When you do, you will be secure.

More from God's Word

If we say, "We have no sin," we are deceiving ourselves, and the truth is not in us. If we confess our sins, He is faithful and righteous to forgive us our sins and to cleanse us from all unrighteousness.

1 John 1:8-9 HCSB

There will be more joy in heaven over one sinner who repents than over 99 righteous people who don't need repentance.

Luke 15:7 HCSB

But the Pharisees and their scribes were complaining to His disciples, "Why do you eat and drink with tax collectors and sinners?" Jesus replied to them, "The healthy don't need a doctor, but the sick do. I have not come to call the righteous, but sinners to repentance."

Luke 5:30-32 HCSB

Fools mock at making restitution, but there is goodwill among the upright.

Proverbs 14:9 HCSB

More Ideas for Your Journey

To do so no more is the truest repentance.

Martin Luther

When true repentance comes, God will not hesitate for a moment to forgive, cast the sins in the sea of forgetfulness, and put the child on the road to restoration.

Beth Moore

Four marks of true repentance are: acknowledgement of wrong, willingness to confess it, willingness to abandon it, and willingness to make restitution.

Corrie ten Boom

A Mother's Prayer

When I stray from Your commandments, Lord, I must not only confess my sins, I must also turn from them. When I fall short, help me to change. When I reject Your Word and Your will for my life, guide me back to Your side. Forgive my sins, Dear Lord, and help me live according to Your plan for my life. Your plan is perfect, Father; I am not. Let me trust in You. Amen

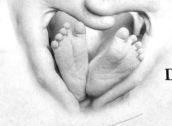

On Sad Days

Why am I so depressed? Why this turmoil within me? Put your hope in God, for I will still praise Him, my Savior and my God.

Psalm 42:11 HCSB

S ome days are light and happy, and some days are not. When we face the inevitable dark days of life, we must choose how we will respond. Will we allow ourselves to sink even more deeply into our own sadness, or will we do the difficult work of pulling ourselves out?

We bring light to the dark days of life by turning first to God, and then to trusted family members and friends. Then, we must go to work solving the problems that confront us. When we do, the clouds will eventually part, and the sun will shine once more upon our souls.

More from God's

Blessed are the poor in spirit, for theirs is kingdom of heaven. Blessed are those who mourn, for shall be comforted.

Matthew - 4 NKJV

Then they cried out to the Lord in their trouble; He saved them from their distress.

Psalm 107:13 HCSB

I assure you: You will weep and wail, but the world will rejoice. You will become sorrowful, but your sorrow will turn to joy.

John 16:20 HCSB

I have heard your prayer, I have seen your tears; surely I will heal you.

2 Kings 20:5 NKJV

May the God of hope fill you with all joy and peace as you trust in him, so that you may overflow with hope by the power of the Holy Spirit.

Romans 15:13 NIV

Ideas for Your Journey

The strengthening of faith comes from staying with it in the _ of trial. We should not shrink from tests of faith.

Catherine Marshall

God is good, and heaven is forever. These two facts should brighten up even the darkest day.

Marie T. Freeman

When life is difficult, God wants us to have a faith that trusts and waits.

Kay Arthur

A Mother's Prayer

Dear Heavenly Father, on those days when I am troubled, You comfort me if I turn my thoughts and prayers to You. When I am afraid, You protect me. When I am discouraged, You lift me up. You are my unending source of strength, Lord. In every circumstance, let me trust Your plan and Your will for my life. Amen

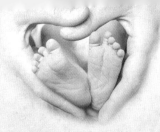

God Is Love

God is love, and the one who remains in love remains in God, and God remains in him.

1 John 4:16 HCSB

The Bible makes this promise: God is love. It's a sweeping statement, a profoundly important description of what God is and how God works. God's love is perfect. When we open our hearts to His perfect love, we are touched by the Creator's hand, and we are transformed.

Today, even if you can only carve out a few quiet moments, offer sincere prayers of thanksgiving to your Creator. He loves you now and throughout all eternity. Open your heart to His presence and His love.

More from God's Word

For God so loved the world, that he gave his only begotten Son, that whosoever believeth in him should not perish, but have everlasting life.

John 3:16 KJV

But the love of the Lord remains forever with those who fear him. His salvation extends to the children's children of those who are faithful to his covenant, of those who obey his commandments!

Psalm 103:17-18 NLT

Praise him, all you people of the earth, for he loves us with unfailing love; the faithfulness of the Lord endures forever. Praise the Lord!

Psalm 117 NLT

But God demonstrates his own love for us in this: While we were still sinners, Christ died for us.

Romans 5:8 NIV

His banner over me was love.

Song of Solomon 2:4 KJV

More Ideas for Your Journey

Let God have you, and let God love you—and don't be surprised if your heart begins to hear music you've never heard and your feet learn to dance as never before.

Max Lucado

I can tell you, from personal experience of walking with God for over fifty years, that He is the Lover of my soul.

Vonette Bright

...God loves these people too, just because they're unattractive or warped in their thinking doesn't mean the Lord doesn't love them.

Ruth Bell Graham

A Mother's Prayer

Dear Lord, the Bible tells me that You are my loving Father. I thank You, Lord, for Your love and for Your Son. Amen

Obedience Now

You must follow the Lord your God and fear Him. You must keep His commands and listen to His voice; you must worship Him and remain faithful to Him.

Deuteronomy 13:4 HCSB

As loving parents, we must teach our children to obey the rules of society and the laws of God. God's laws are contained in a guidebook for righteous living called the Holy Bible. It contains thorough instructions which, if followed, lead to fulfillment, peace, righteousness, and salvation. But, if we choose to ignore God's commandments, the results are as predictable as they are tragic.

Talking about obedience is easy; living obediently is considerably harder. But, if we are to be responsible role models for our families and friends, we must study God's Word and obey it.

Phillips Brooks advised, "Be such a person, and live such a life, that if every person were such as you, and every life a life like yours, this earth would be God's

Paradise." And that's sound advice because our families and friends are watching . . . and so, for that matter, is God.

More from God's Word

Therefore, get your minds ready for action, being self-disciplined, and set your hope completely on the grace to be brought to you at the revelation of Jesus Christ. As obedient children, do not be conformed to the desires of your former ignorance but, as the One who called you is holy, you also are to be holy in all your conduct.

1 Peter 1:13-15 HCSB

But whoever keeps His word, truly the love of God is perfected in him. By this we know that we are in Him. He who says he abides in Him ought himself also to walk just as He walked.

1 John 2:5-6 NKJV

Because the eyes of the Lord are on the righteous and His ears are open to their request. But the face of the Lord is against those who do evil.

1 Peter 3:12 HCSB

More Ideas for Your Journey

There are two things we are called to do: we are to depend on His strength and be obedient to His Word. If we can't handle being dependent and obedient, we will never become the kind of people who have a heart for God.

Stuart Briscoe

God is God. Because He is God, He is worthy of my trust and obedience. I will find rest nowhere but in His holy will, a will that is unspeakably beyond my largest notions of what He is up to.

Elisabeth Elliot

The pathway of obedience can sometimes be difficult, but it always leads to a strengthening of our inner woman.

Vonette Bright

A Mother's Prayer

Dear Lord, make me a mother who is obedient to Your Word. Let me live according to Your commandments. Direct my path far from the temptations and distractions of this world. And, let me discover Your will and follow it, Lord, this day and always. Amen

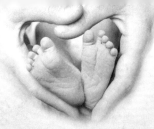

Walking with the Wise

Listen to advice and accept correction, and in the end you will be wise.

Proverbs 19:20 NCV

Do you wish to become wise? Then you must walk with people who, by their words and their presence, make you wiser. And, to the best of your ability, you must avoid those people who encourage you to think foolish thoughts or do foolish things.

Today, as a gift to yourself, select, from your friends and family members, a mentor whose judgement you trust. Then listen carefully to your mentor's advice and be willing to accept that advice, even if accepting it requires effort, or pain, or both. Consider your mentor to be God's gift to you. Thank God for that gift, and use it.

More Ideas for Your Journey

The next best thing to being wise oneself is to live in a circle of those who are.

C. S. Lewis

It takes a wise person to give good advice, but an even wiser person to take it.

Marie T. Freeman

No matter how crazy or nutty your life has seemed, God can make something strong and good out of it. He can help you grow wide branches for others to use as shelter.

Barbara Johnson

A Mother's Prayer

Dear Lord, thank You for family members, for friends, and for mentors. When I am troubled, let me turn to them for help, for guidance, for comfort, and for perspective. And Father, let me be a friend and mentor to others, so that my love for You may be reflected in my genuine concern for them. Amen

Observing the Sabbath

Remember the Sabbath day, to keep it holy.

Exodus 20:8 NKJV

When God gave Moses the Ten Commandments, it became perfectly clear that our Heavenly Father intends for us to make the Sabbath a holy day, a day for worship, for contemplation, for fellowship, and for rest. Yet we live in a seven-day-a-week world, a world that all too often treats Sunday as a regular workday.

How does your family observe the Lord's day? When church is over, do you treat Sunday like any other day of the week? If so, it's time to think long and hard about your family's schedule and your family's priorities.

Whenever we ignore God's commandments, we pay a price. So if you've been treating Sunday as just another day, it's time to break that habit. When Sunday rolls around, don't try to fill every spare moment. Take time to rest . . . Father's orders!

More Ideas for Your Journey

God asks that we worship Him with our concentrated minds as well as with our wills and emotions. A divided and scattered mind is not effective.

Catherine Marshall

God has promised to give you all of eternity. The least you can do is give Him one day a week in return.

Marie T. Freeman

Praise Him! Praise Him! / Tell of His excellent greatness. / Praise Him! Praise Him! / Ever in joyful song!

Fanny Crosby

A Mother's Prayer

Dear Lord, I thank You for the Sabbath day, a day when my family and I can worship You and praise Your Son. We will keep the Sabbath as a holy day, a day when we can honor You. Amen

The Beauty of Humility

For everyone who exalts himself will be humbled, and the one who humbles himself will be exalted.

Luke 14:11 HCSB

Humility is not, in most cases, a naturally occurring human trait. Most of us, it seems, are more than willing to overestimate our own accomplishments. We are tempted to say, "Look how wonderful I am!" . . . hoping all the while that the world will agree with our own self-appraisals.

God honors humility . . . and He rewards those who humbly serve Him. When we acquired the wisdom to be humble, we bring enlightenment to the world (and blessings to ourselves).

But if we cannot overcome the tendency to overestimate our own accomplishments, then God still has some important lessons to teach us—lessons about the wisdom, the power, and the beauty of humility.

More from God's Word

Clothe yourselves with humility toward one another, because God resists the proud, but gives grace to the humble.

1 Peter 5:5 HCSB

But He said to me, "My grace is sufficient for you, for power is perfected in weakness." Therefore, I will most gladly boast all the more about my weaknesses, so that Christ's power may reside in me.

2 Corinthians 12:9 HCSB

You will save the humble people; but Your eyes are on the haughty, that You may bring them down.

2 Samuel 22:28 NKJV

If My people who are called by My name will humble themselves, and pray and seek My face, and turn from their wicked ways, then I will hear from heaven, and will forgive their sin and heal their land.

2 Chronicles 7:14 NKJV

Do nothing out of rivalry or conceit, but in humility consider others as more important than yourselves.

Philippians 2:3 HCSB

More Ideas for Your Journey

If you know who you are in Christ, your personal ego is not an issue.

Beth Moore

The humble person will not be thinking of humility: He will not be thinking about himself at all.

C. S. Lewis

We are never stronger than the moment we admit we are weak.

Beth Moore

Humility is the fairest and rarest flower that blooms.

Charles Swindoll

A Mother's Prayer

Lord, You are great, and I am human. Keep me humble, and keep me mindful that all my gifts come from You. Amen

Too Many Distractions?

Let us lay aside every weight and the sin that so easily ensnares us, and run with endurance the race that lies before us, keeping our eyes on Jesus, the source and perfecter of our faith.

Hebrews 12:1-2 HCSB

All of us must live through those days when the traffic jams, the computer crashes, and the dog makes a main course out of our homework. But, when we find ourselves distracted by the minor frustrations of life, we must catch ourselves, take a deep breath, and lift our thoughts upward.

Although we may, at times, struggle mightily to rise above the distractions of the everyday living, we need never struggle alone. God is here—eternal and faithful, with infinite patience and love—and, if we reach out to Him, He will restore our sense of perspective and give peace to our souls.

More from God's Word

Let your eyes look forward; fix your gaze straight ahead.

Proverbs 4:25 HCSB

Enter through the narrow gate; because the gate is wide and the road is broad that leads to destruction, and there are many who go through it. How narrow is the gate and difficult the road that leads to life; and few find it.

Matthew 7:13-14 HCSB

Teach me, O Lord, the way of Your statutes, and I shall keep it to the end.

Psalm 119:33 NKJV

Don't abandon wisdom, and she will watch over you; love her, and she will guard you.

Proverbs 4:6 HCSB

The one who follows instruction is on the path to life, but the one who rejects correction goes astray.

Proverbs 10:17 HCSB

More Ideas for Your Journey

Setting goals is one way you can be sure that you will focus your efforts on the main things so that trivial matters will not become your focus.

Charles Stanley

When Jesus is in our midst, He brings His limitless power along as well. But, Jesus must be in the middle, all eyes and hearts focused on Him.

Shirley Dobson

We need to stop focusing on our lacks and stop giving out excuses and start looking at and listening to Jesus.

Anne Graham Lotz

A Mother's Prayer

Dear Lord, help me to face this day with a spirit of optimism and thanksgiving. And let me focus my thoughts on You and Your incomparable gifts. Amen

Your Real Treasures

I will bless them and the places surrounding my hill. I will send down showers in season; there will be showers of blessings.

Ezekiel 34:26 NIV

Because you are a mother, you have been specially blessed by the Creator. God has given you blessings that are, in truth, simply too numerous to count. Your blessings include life, family, freedom, friends, talents, and possessions, for starters. But, your greatest blessing—a priceless treasure that is yours for the asking—is God's gift of salvation through Christ Jesus.

The gifts you receive from God are multiplied when you share them with others. Today, give thanks to God for your blessings and demonstrate your gratitude by sharing those blessings with your family, with your friends, and with the world.

More from God's Word

The Lord bless you and keep you; the Lord make His face shine upon you, and be gracious to you.

Numbers 6:24-25 NKJV

You will show me the path of life; in Your presence is fullness of joy; at Your right hand are pleasures forevermore.

Psalm 16:11 NKJV

Obey My voice, and I will be your God, and you shall be my people. And walk in all the ways that I have commanded you, that it may be well with you.

Jeremiah 7:23 NKJV

I have come that they may have life, and that they may have it more abundantly.

John 10:10 NKJV

Until now you have asked for nothing in My name. Ask and you will receive, that your joy may be complete.

John 16:24 HCSB

More Ideas for Your Journey

Do we not continually pass by blessings innumerable without notice, and instead fix our eyes on what we feel to be our trials and our losses, and think and talk about these until our whole horizon is filled with them, and we almost begin to think we have no blessings at all?

Hannah Whitall Smith

When you and I are related to Jesus Christ, our strength and wisdom and peace and joy and love and hope may run out, but His life rushes in to keep us filled to the brim. We are showered with blessings, not because of anything we have or have not done, but simply because of Him.

Anne Graham Lotz

A Mother's Prayer

Lord, let me be a mother who counts her blessings, and let me be Your faithful servant as I give praise to the Giver of all things good. You have richly blessed my life, Lord. Let me, in turn, be a blessing to my family and my world—and may the glory be Yours forever. Amen

He Is Sufficient

And He said to me, "My grace is sufficient for you, for My strength is made perfect in weakness."

2 Corinthians 12:9 NKJV

Of this you can be certain: God is sufficient to meet your needs. Period.

Do the demands of motherhood seem overwhelming at times? If so, you must learn to rely not only upon your own resources, but also upon the promises of your Father in heaven. God will hold your hand and walk with you and your family if you let Him. So even if your circumstances are difficult, trust the Father.

The Psalmist writes, "Weeping may endure for a night, but joy comes in the morning" (Psalm 30:5 NKJV). But when we are suffering, the morning may seem very far away. It is not. God promises that He is "near to those who have a broken heart" (Psalm 34:18 NKJV). When we are troubled, we must turn to Him, and we must encourage our friends and family members to do likewise.

If you are discouraged by the inevitable demands of life here on earth, be mindful of this fact: the loving heart of God is sufficient to meet any challenge . . . including yours.

More from God's Word

And my God shall supply all your need according to His riches in glory by Christ Jesus.

Philippians 4:19 NKJV

The LORD is my strength and my song; he has become my victory. He is my God, and I will praise him.

Exodus 15:2 NLT

Every word of God is flawless; he is a shield to those who take refuge in him.

Proverbs 30:5 NIV

Finally, my brethren, be strong in the Lord and in the power of His might. Put on the whole armor of God, that you may be able to stand against the wiles of the devil.

Ephesians 6:10-11 NKJV

More Ideas for Your Journey

Yes, God's grace is always sufficient, and His arms are always open to give it. But, will our arms be open to receive it?

Beth Moore

I grew up learning to be self-reliant, but now, to grow up in Christ, I must unlearn self-reliance and learn self-distrust in light of his all-sufficiency.

Mary Morrison Suggs

God's saints in all ages have realized that God was enough for them. God is enough for time; God is enough for eternity. God is enough!

Hannah Whitall Smith

A Mother's Prayer

Dear Lord, as I face the challenges of this day, You protect me. I thank You, Father, for Your love and for Your strength. I will lean upon You today and forever. Amen

Your Thoughts

Fix your thoughts on what is true and honorable and right.
Think about things that are pure and lovely and admirable.
Think about things that are excellent and worthy of praise.

Philippians 4:8 NLT

Thoughts are intensely powerful things. Our thoughts have the power to lift us up or drag us down; they have the power to energize us or deplete us, to inspire us to greater accomplishments or to make those accomplishments impossible.

How will you and your family members direct your thoughts today? Will you obey the words of Philippians 4:8 by dwelling upon those things that are honorable, true, and worthy of praise? Or will you allow your thoughts to be hijacked by the negativity that seems to dominate our troubled world?

Are you fearful, angry, bored, or worried? Are you so preoccupied with the concerns of this day that you fail to thank God for the promise of eternity? Are you confused, bitter, or pessimistic? If so, God wants to have a little talk with you.

God intends that you experience joy and abundance, but He will not force His joy upon you; you must claim it for yourself. It's up to you and your loved ones to celebrate the life that God has given you by focusing your minds upon "whatever is commendable." So form the habit of spending more time thinking about your blessings and less time fretting about your hardships. Then, take time to thank the Giver of all things good for gifts that are, in truth, far too numerous to count.

More from God's Word

Set your minds on what is above, not on what is on the earth.

Colossians 3:2 HCSB

Commit your works to the Lord, and your thoughts will be established.

Proverbs 16:3 NKJV

Guard your heart above all else, for it is the source of life.

Proverbs 4:23 HCSB

May the words of my mouth and the meditation of my heart be acceptable to You, Lord, my rock and my Redeemer.

Psalm 19:14 HCSB

More Ideas for Your Journey

Every major spiritual battle is in the mind.

Charles Stanley

The things we think are the things that feed our souls. If we think on pure and lovely things, we shall grow pure and lovely like them; and the converse is equally true.

Hannah Whitall Smith

I became aware of one very important concept I had missed before: my attitude—not my circumstances—was what was making me unhappy.

Vonette Bright

A Mother's Prayer

Dear Lord, I will focus on Your love, Your power, Your promises, and Your Son. When I am weak, I will turn to You for strength; when I am worried, I will turn to You for comfort; when I am troubled, I will turn to You for patience and perspective. Help me guard my thoughts, Lord, so that I may honor You this day and forever. Amen

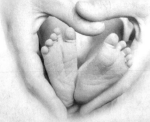

The Ultimate Protection

*The Lord is my rock, my fortress, and my deliverer, my
God, my mountain where I seek refuge. My shield, the horn
of my salvation, my stronghold, my refuge, and my Savior.*

2 Samuel 22:2-3 HCSB

As a busy woman, you know from firsthand experience that life is not always easy. But as a recipient of God's grace, you also know that you are protected by a loving Heavenly Father.

In times of trouble, God will comfort you; in times of sorrow, He will dry your tears. When you are troubled, or weak, or sorrowful, God is neither distant nor disinterested. To the contrary, God is always present and always vitally engaged in the events of your life. Reach out to Him, and build your future on the rock that cannot be shaken . . . trust in God and rely upon His provisions. He can provide everything you really need . . . and far, far more.

More from God's Word

For the LORD your God has arrived to live among you. He is a mighty Savior. He will rejoice over you with great gladness. With his love, he will calm all your fears. He will exult over you by singing a happy song.

Zephaniah 3:17 HCSB

God—His way is perfect; the word of the Lord is pure. He is a shield to all who take refuge in Him.

Psalm 18:30 HCSB

The Lord is my rock, my fortress, and my deliverer.

Psalm 18:2 HCSB

The Lord bless you and protect you; the Lord make His face shine on you, and be gracious to you.

Numbers 6:24-25 HCSB

I know whom I have believed and am persuaded that He is able to guard what has been entrusted to me until that day.

2 Timothy 1:12 HCSB

More Ideas for Your Journey

He goes before us, follows behind us, and hems us safe inside the realm of His protection.

Beth Moore

Prayer is our pathway not only to divine protection, but also to a personal, intimate relationship with God.

Shirley Dobson

The Will of God will never take you where the Grace of God will not protect you.

Anonymous

A Mother's Prayer

Lord, You have promised to protect me, and I will trust You. Today, I will live courageously as I place my hopes, my faith, and life in Your hands. Let my life be a testimony to the transforming power of Your love, Your grace, and Your Son. Amen

The Right Kind of Fear

The fear of the Lord is the beginning of knowledge, but fools despise wisdom and discipline.

Proverbs 1:7 NIV

A re you a woman who possesses a healthy, fearful respect for God's power? Hopefully so. After all, God's Word teaches that the fear of the Lord is the beginning of knowledge (Proverbs 1:7).

When we fear the Creator—and when we honor Him by obeying His commandments—we receive God's approval and His blessings. But, when we ignore Him or disobey His commandments, we invite disastrous consequences.

God's hand shapes the universe, and it shapes our lives. God maintains absolute sovereignty over His creation, and His power is beyond comprehension. The fear of the Lord is, indeed, the beginning of knowledge. But thankfully, once we possess a healthy, reverent fear of God, we need never be fearful of anything else.

More from God's Word

To fear the Lord is to hate evil.

Proverbs 8:13 HCSB

The fear of the Lord is the beginning of wisdom, and the knowledge of the Holy One is understanding.

Proverbs 9:10 HCSB

The fear of the Lord is the beginning of wisdom; all who follow His instructions have good insight.

Psalm 111:10 HCSB

The fear of the Lord is a fountain of life, turning people from the snares of death.

Proverbs 14:27 HCSB

Don't consider yourself to be wise; fear the Lord and turn away from evil.

Proverbs 3:7 HCSB

More Ideas for Your Journey

The remarkable thing about fearing God is that when you fear God, you fear nothing else, whereas if you do not fear God, you fear everything else.

Oswald Chambers

When true believers are awed by the greatness of God and by the privilege of becoming His children, then they become sincerely motivated, effective evangelists.

Bill Hybels

The fear of God is the death of every other fear.

C. H. Spurgeon

A Mother's Prayer

Dear Lord, others have expectations of me, and I have hopes and desires for my life. Lord, bring all other expectations in line with Your plans for me. May my only fear be that of displeasing the One who created me. May I obey Your commandments and seek Your will this day and every day. Amen

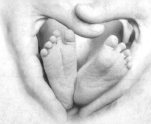

God's Abundance

I came that they may have life, and have it abundantly.

John 10:10 NASB

A re you the kind of mom who accepts God's spiritual abundance without reservation? If so, you are availing yourself of the peace and the joy that He has promised. Do you sincerely seek the riches that our Savior offers to those who give themselves to Him? Then follow Him. When you do, you will receive the love and the abundance that Jesus offers to those who follow Him.

Seek first the salvation that is available through a personal, passionate relationship with Christ, and then claim the joy, the peace, and the spiritual abundance that the Shepherd offers His sheep.

More from God's Word

And God is able to make every grace overflow to you, so that in every way, always having everything you need, you may excel in every good work.

2 Corinthians 9:8 HCSB

Until now you have asked for nothing in My name. Ask and you will receive, that your joy may be complete.

John 16:24 HCSB

Come to terms with God and be at peace; in this way good will come to you.

Job 22:21 HCSB

My cup runs over. Surely goodness and mercy shall follow me all the days of my life; and I will dwell in the house of the Lord forever.

Psalm 23:5-6 NKJV

And He said to them, "Take heed and beware of covetousness, for one's life does not consist in the abundance of the things he possesses."

Luke 12:15 NKJV

More Ideas for Your Journey

If we were given all we wanted here, our hearts would settle for this world rather than the next.

Elisabeth Elliot

Jesus intended for us to be overwhelmed by the blessings of regular days. He said it was the reason he had come: "I am come that they might have life, and that they might have it more abundantly."

Gloria Gaither

God is the giver, and we are the receivers. And His richest gifts are bestowed not upon those who do the greatest things, but upon those who accept His abundance and His grace.

Hannah Whitall Smith

A Mother's Prayer

Dear Lord, You have offered me the gift of abundance through Your Son. Thank You, Father, for the abundant life that is mine through Christ Jesus. Let me accept His gifts and use them always to glorify You. Amen

Beyond Worry

Let not your heart be troubled; you believe in God, believe also in Me.

John 14:1 NKJV

If you are like most mothers, it is simply a fact of life: from time to time, you worry. You worry about children, about health, about finances, about safety, and about countless other challenges of life, some great and some small. Where is the best place to take your worries? Take them to God. Take your troubles to Him, and your fears, and your sorrows.

Barbara Johnson correctly observed, "Worry is the senseless process of cluttering up tomorrow's opportunities with leftover problems from today." So if you'd like to make the most out of this day (and every one hereafter), turn your worries over to a Power greater than yourself . . . and spend your valuable time and energy solving the problems you can fix . . . while trusting God to do the rest.

More Ideas for Your Journey

Much that worries us beforehand can, quite unexpectedly, have a happy and simple solution. Worries just don't matter. Things really are in a better hand than ours.

Dietrich Bonhoeffer

Today is mine. Tomorrow is none of my business. If I peer anxiously into the fog of the future, I will strain my spiritual eyes so that I will not see clearly what is required of me now.

Elisabeth Elliott

The beginning of anxiety is the end of faith, and the beginning of true faith is the end of anxiety.

George Mueller

A Mother's Prayer

Dear Lord, wherever I find myself, let me celebrate more and worry less. When my faith begins to waver, help me to trust You more. Then, with praise on my lips and the love of Your Son in my heart, let me live courageously, faithfully, prayerfully, and thankfully this day and every day. Amen

A Willingness to Serve

Whoever wants to become great among you must serve the rest of you like a servant.

Matthew 20:26 NCV

Jesus teaches that the most esteemed men and women are not the leaders of society or the captains of industry. To the contrary, Jesus teaches that the greatest among us are those who choose to minister and to serve.

Today, you may feel the temptation to build yourself up in the eyes of your neighbors. Resist that temptation. Instead, serve your neighbors quietly and without fanfare. Find a need and fill it . . . humbly. Lend a helping hand and share a word of kindness . . . anonymously.

Today, take the time to minister to those in need. Then, when you have done your best to serve your neighbors and to serve your God, you can rest comfortably knowing that in the eyes of God you have achieved greatness. And God's eyes, after all, are the only ones that really count.

More from God's Word

A person should consider us in this way: as servants of Christ and managers of God's mysteries. In this regard, it is expected of managers that each one be found faithful.

1 Corinthians 4:1-2 HCSB

If they serve Him obediently, they will end their days in prosperity and their years in happiness.

Job 36:11 HCSB

We must do the works of Him who sent Me while it is day. Night is coming when no one can work.

John 9:4 HCSB

Serve the Lord with gladness.

Psalm 100:2 HCSB

If anyone serves Me, let him follow Me; and where I am, there My servant will be also. If anyone serves Me, him My Father will honor.

John 12:26 NKJV

More Ideas for Your Journey

Christianity, in its purest form, is nothing more than seeing Jesus. Christian service, in its purest form, is nothing more than imitating him who we see. To see his Majesty and to imitate him: that is the sum of Christianity.

Max Lucado

So many times we say that we can't serve God because we aren't whatever is needed. We're not talented enough or smart enough or whatever. But if you are in covenant with Jesus Christ, He is responsible for covering your weaknesses, for being your strength. He will give you His abilities for your disabilities!

Kay Arthur

A Mother's Prayer

Dear Lord, as a mother, I am an example to every member of my family. Give me a servant's heart and make me a faithful steward of my gifts. Let me follow in the footsteps of Your Son Jesus who taught us by example that to be great in Your eyes, Lord, is to serve others humbly, faithfully, and lovingly. Amen

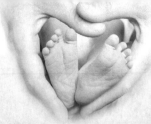

God's Good News

But God, who is abundant in mercy, because of His great love that He had for us, made us alive with the Messiah even though we were dead in trespasses. By grace you are saved!

Ephesians 2:4-5 HCSB

Christ died on the cross so that we might have eternal life. This gift, freely given from God's only Son, is the priceless possession of everyone who accepts Him as Lord and Savior.

Thankfully, God's grace is not an earthly reward for righteous behavior; it is, instead, a blessed spiritual gift. When we accept Christ into our hearts, we are saved by His grace. The familiar words from the book of Ephesians make God's promise perfectly clear: "For it is by grace you have been saved, through faith—and this not from yourselves, it is the gift of God—not by works, so that no one can boast" (2:8-9 NIV).

God's grace is the ultimate gift, and we owe Him our eternal gratitude. Our Heavenly Father is waiting patiently for each of us to accept His Son and receive

His grace. Let us accept that gift today so that we might enjoy God's presence now and throughout all eternity.

More from God's Word

My grace is sufficient for you, for My strength is made perfect in weakness.

2 Corinthians 12:9 NKJV

And we have seen and testify that the Father has sent the Son as Savior of the world.

1 John 4:14 NKJV

For all have sinned and fall short of the glory of God, and are justified freely by his grace through the redemption that came by Christ Jesus.

Romans 3:23-24 NIV

In Him we have redemption through His blood, the forgiveness of our trespasses, according to the riches of His grace that He lavished on us with all wisdom and understanding.

Ephesians 1:7-8 HCSB

More Ideas for Your Journey

No one is beyond his grace. No situation, anywhere on earth, is too hard for God.

Jim Cymbala

God does amazing works through prayers that seek to extend His grace to others.

Shirley Dobson

In your greatest weakness, turn to your greatest strength, Jesus, and hear Him say, "My grace is sufficient for you, for My strength is made perfect in weakness" (2 Corinthians 12:9, NKJV).

Lisa Whelchel

A Mother's Prayer

Accepting Your grace can be hard, Lord. Somehow, I feel that I must earn Your love and Your acceptance. Yet, the Bible promises that You love me and save me by Your grace. It is a gift I can only accept and cannot earn. Thank You for Your priceless, everlasting gift. Amen

Beyond Negativity

Don't criticize one another, brothers. He who criticizes a brother or judges his brother criticizes the law and judges the law. But if you judge the law, you are not a doer of the law but a judge.

James 4:11 HCSB

From experience, we know that it is easier to criticize than to correct; we understand that it is easier to find faults than solutions; and we realize that excessive criticism is usually destructive, not productive. Yet the urge to criticize others remains a powerful temptation for most of us. Our task, as obedient believers, is to break the twin habits of negative thinking and critical speech.

Negativity is highly contagious: we give it to others who, in turn, give it back to us. This cycle can be broken by positive thoughts, heartfelt prayers, and encouraging words. As thoughtful servants of a loving God, we can use the transforming power of Christ's love to break the chains of negativity. And we should.

More from God's Word

Whoever shows contempt for his neighbor lacks sense, but a man with understanding keeps silent.

Proverbs 11:12 HCSB

But now you must also put away all the following: anger, wrath, malice, slander, and filthy language from your mouth.

Colossians 3:8 HCSB

My dearly loved brothers, understand this: everyone must be quick to hear, slow to speak, and slow to anger, for man's anger does not accomplish God's righteousness.

James 1:19-20 HCSB

All bitterness, anger and wrath, insult and slander must be removed from you, along with all wickedness. And be kind and compassionate to one another, forgiving one another, just as God also forgave you in Christ.

Ephesians 4:31-32 HCSB

Kind people do themselves a favor, but cruel people bring trouble on themselves.

Proverbs 11:17 NCV

More Ideas for Your Journey

I still believe we ought to talk about Jesus. The old country doctor of my boyhood days always began his examination by saying, "Let me see your tongue." That's a good way to check a Christian: the tongue test. Let's hear what he is talking about.

Vance Havner

Judging draws the judgment of others.

Catherine Marshall

Being critical of others, including God, is one way we try to avoid facing and judging our own sins.

Warren Wiersbe

A Mother's Prayer

Help me, Lord, rise above the need to criticize others. May my own shortcomings humble me, and may I always be a source of genuine encouragement to my family and friends. Amen

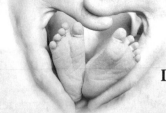

Big Dreams

But as it is written: What no eye has seen and no ear has heard, and what has never come into a man's heart, is what God has prepared for those who love Him.

1 Corinthians 2:9 HCSB

Are you willing to entertain the possibility that God has big plans in store for you and your family? Hopefully so. Yet sometimes, especially if you've recently experienced a life-altering disappointment, you may find it difficult to envision a brighter future for yourself and your family. If so, it's time to reconsider your own capabilities . . . and God's.

Your Heavenly Father created you with unique gifts and untapped talents; your job is to tap them. When you do, you'll begin to feel an increasing sense of confidence in yourself and in your future.

It takes courage to dream big dreams. You will discover that courage when you do three things: accept the past, trust God to handle the future, and make the most of the time He has given you today.

Nothing is too difficult for God, and no dreams are too big for Him—not even yours. So start living—and dreaming—accordingly.

More from God's Word

Looking at them, Jesus said, "With men it is impossible, but not with God, because all things are possible with God."

Mark 10:27 HCSB

Now may the God of hope fill you with all joy and peace in believing, so that you may overflow with hope by the power of the Holy Spirit.

Romans 15:13 HCSB

Where there is no vision, the people perish....

Proverbs 29:18 KJV

Live full lives, full in the fullness of God. God can do anything, you know—far more than you could ever imagine or guess or request in your wildest dreams! He does it not by pushing us around but by working within us, his Spirit deeply and gently within us.

Ephesians 3:19-20 MSG

More Ideas for Your Journey

You cannot out-dream God.

John Eldredge

The future lies all before us. Shall it only be a slight advance upon what we usually do? Ought it not to be a bound, a leap forward to altitudes of endeavor and success undreamed of before?

Annie Armstrong

Allow your dreams a place in your prayers and plans. God-given dreams can help you move into the future He is preparing for you.

Barbara Johnson

A Mother's Prayer

Dear Lord, give me the courage to dream and the faithfulness to trust in Your perfect plan. When I am worried or weary, give me strength for today and hope for tomorrow. Keep me mindful of Your healing power, Your infinite love, and Your eternal salvation. Amen

Your Testimony

And I say to you, anyone who acknowledges Me before men, the Son of Man will also acknowledge him before the angels of God; but whoever denies Me before men will be denied before the angels of God.

Luke 12:8-9 HCSB

In his second letter to Timothy, Paul offers a message to believers of every generation when he writes, "God has not given us a spirit of timidity" (1:7 NASB). Paul's meaning is crystal clear: When sharing our testimonies, we, as Christians, must be courageous, forthright, and unashamed.

We live in a world that desperately needs the healing message of Christ Jesus. Every believer, each in his or her own way, bears a personal responsibility for sharing that message. If you are a believer in Christ, you know how He has touched your heart and changed your life. Now it's your turn to share the Good News with others. And remember: today is the perfect time to share your testimony because tomorrow may quite simply be too late.

More from God's Word

But sanctify the Lord God in your hearts, and always be ready to give a defense to everyone who asks you a reason for the hope that is in you.

1 Peter 3:15 HCSB

The following night, the Lord stood by him and said, "Have courage! For as you have testified about Me in Jerusalem, so you must also testify in Rome."

Acts 23:11 HCSB

But as for me, I will never boast about anything except the cross of our Lord Jesus Christ, through whom the world has been crucified to me, and I to the world.

Galatians 6:14 HCSB

You are the light of the world. A city that is set on a hill cannot be hidden. Nor do they light a lamp and put it under a basket, but on a lampstand, and it gives light to all who are in the house. Let your light so shine before men, that they may see your good works and glorify your Father in heaven.

Matthew 5:14–16 NKJV

More Ideas for Your Journey

Claim the joy that is yours. Pray. And know that your joy is used by God to reach others.

Kay Arthur

There is nothing anybody else can do that can stop God from using us. We can turn everything into a testimony.

Corrie ten Boom

Faith in small things has repercussions that ripple all the way out. In a huge, dark room a little match can light up the place.

Joni Eareckson Tada

A Mother's Prayer

Lord, the life that I live and the words that I speak will tell my family and the world how I feel about You. Today and every day, let my testimony be worthy of You. Let my words be sure and true, and let my actions point others to You. Amen

Today's Decisions

The righteous one will live by his faith.

Habakkuk 2:4 HCSB

God has given us a guidebook for righteous living called the Holy Bible. It contains thorough instructions which, if followed, lead to fulfillment, righteousness, and salvation. But, if we choose to ignore God's commandments, the results are as predictable as they are tragic.

The Bible instructs us that a righteous life has many components: faith, honesty, generosity, love, kindness, humility, gratitude, and worship, to name but a few. And, if we seek to follow the steps of our Savior, Jesus Christ, we must, to the best of our abilities, live according to the principles contained in God's Holy Word.

As a loving mother, you are keenly aware that God has entrusted you with a profound responsibility: caring for the needs of your family, including their spiritual needs. To fulfill that responsibility, you must study God's Word and live by it. When you do, your example will be a blessing not only to your loved ones, but also to generations yet unborn.

More from God's Word

Because the eyes of the Lord are on the righteous and His ears are open to their request. But the face of the Lord is against those who do evil.

1 Peter 3:12 HCSB

Therefore, come out from among them and be separate, says the Lord; do not touch any unclean thing, and I will welcome you.

2 Corinthians 6:17 HCSB

Flee from youthful passions, and pursue righteousness, faith, love, and peace, along with those who call on the Lord from a pure heart.

2 Timothy 2:22 HCSB

Do what is right and good in the Lord's sight, so that you may prosper and so that you may enter and possess the good land the Lord your God swore to [give] your fathers.

Deuteronomy 6:18 HCSB

More Ideas for Your Journey

Righteousness comes only from God.

Kay Arthur

When we do what is right, we have contentment, peace, and happiness.

Beverly LaHaye

Holiness is not an impossibility for any of us.

Elisabeth Elliot

A Mother's Prayer

Dear Lord, let me obey Your Word, and let me teach my children to do the same. Make me a mother who obeys Your commandments, and let me walk righteously in the footsteps of Your Son, today and every day. Amen

Your Wonderful Life

I have set before you life and death, blessing and curse. Choose life so that you and your descendants may live, love the Lord your God, obey Him, and remain faithful to Him. For He is your life, and He will prolong your life in the land the Lord swore to give to your fathers Abraham, Isaac, and Jacob.

Deuteronomy 30:19-20 HCSB

Each day, as we awaken from sleep and begin the new day, we are confronted with countless opportunities to serve God and to worship Him. When we do, He blesses us. But, if we turn our backs to the Creator, or, if we are simply too busy to acknowledge His greatness, we do ourselves a profound disservice.

As women in a fast-changing world, we face challenges that sometimes leave us feeling overworked, overcommitted, and overwhelmed. But God has different plans for us. He intends that we take time each day to slow down long enough to praise Him and glorify His Son. When we do, our spirits are calmed and our lives are enriched, as are the lives of our families and friends.

Each day provides a glorious opportunity to place ourselves in the service of the One who is the Giver of all blessings. May we seek His will, trust His word, and place Him where He belongs: at the center of our lives.

More from God's Word

He who follows righteousness and mercy finds life, righteousness and honor.

Proverbs 21:21 NKJV

I urge you now to live the life to which God called you.

Ephesians 4:1 NKJV

Shout triumphantly to the Lord, all the earth. Serve the Lord with gladness; come before Him with joyful songs.

Psalm 100:1-2 HCSB

Jesus told him, "I am the way, the truth, and the life. No one comes to the Father except through Me."

John 14:6 HCSB

More Ideas for Your Journey

Life is a glorious opportunity.

Billy Graham

The Christian life is motivated, not by a list of do's and don'ts, but by the gracious outpouring of God's love and blessing.

Anne Graham Lotz

Life is simply hard. That's all there is to it. Thank goodness, the intensity of difficulty rises and falls. Some seasons are far more bearable than others, but none is without challenge.

Beth Moore

A Mother's Prayer

Lord, You have given me the gift of life. Let me treasure it, and let me use it for Your service and for Your glory. Amen

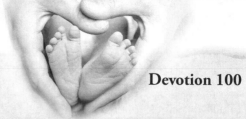

How Much Love?

We know how much God loves us, and we have put our trust in him. God is love, and all who live in love live in God, and God lives in them.

1 John 4:16 NLT

As a mother, you know the profound love that you hold in your heart for your own children. As a child of God, you can only imagine the infinite love that your Heavenly Father holds for you.

God made you in His own image and gave you salvation through the person of His Son Jesus Christ. And now, precisely because you are a wondrous creation treasured by God, a question presents itself: What will you do in response to the Creator's love? Will you ignore it or embrace it? Will you return it or neglect it? That decision, of course, is yours and yours alone.

When you embrace God's love, you are forever changed. When you embrace God's love, you feel differently about yourself, your neighbors, your family, and your world. More importantly, you share God's message—and His love—with others.

Your Heavenly Father—a God of infinite love and mercy—is waiting to embrace you with open arms. Accept His love today and forever.

More from God's Word

We love Him because He first loved us.

1 John 4:19 NKJV

Draw near to God, and He will draw near to you.

James 4:8 HCSB

For He is gracious and compassionate, slow to anger, rich in faithful love.

Joel 2:13 HCSB

For God loved the world in this way: He gave His only Son, so that everyone who believes in Him will not perish but have eternal life.

John 3:16 HCSB

For the Lord is good, and His love is eternal; His faithfulness endures through all generations.

Psalm 100:5 HCSB

More Ideas for Your Journey

God wants to reveal Himself as your heavenly Father. When you are hurting, you can run to Him and crawl up into His lap. When you wonder which way to turn, you can grasp His strong hand, and He'll guide you along life's path. When everything around you is falling apart, you'll feel your Father's arm around your shoulder to hold you together.

Lisa Whelchel

Jesus loves us with fidelity, purity, constancy, and passion, no matter how imperfect we are.

Stormie Omartian

Nails didn't hold Jesus on the cross. His love for you did.

Anonymous

A Mother's Prayer

Thank You, Dear God, for Your love. You are my loving Father—help me to be a loving mother. You are my Creator: I will praise You; I will worship You; and I will love You . . . today, tomorrow, and forever. Amen